RADICAL LIBERATION THEOLOGY:
AN
EVANGELICAL RESPONSE

RADICAL LIBERATION THEOLOGY:
AN
EVANGELICAL RESPONSE

RAYMOND C. HUNDLEY

B BRISTOL
BOOKS
WILMORE, KY 40390

RADICAL LIBERATION THEOLOGY:
An Evangelical Response
Copyright © 1987 by OMS International, Inc.
Published by Bristol Books

First Printing, September 1987
Second Printing, August 1989

All Scripture quotations are from the *New American Standard Bible*, © 1960, 1962, 1963, 1968, 1971, 1972, 1973, 1975, 1977 by The Lockman Foundation.

Library of Congress Card Number: 87-71848
ISBN: 0-917851-42-0
Suggested Subject Headings:
  1. Liberation Theology
  2. Theology, Doctrinal—Latin America
Recommended Dewey Decimal Classification: 230

BRISTOL BOOKS
An imprint of Good News, Forum for Scriptural Christianity, Inc.
308 East Main Street • Wilmore, Kentucky 40390

Dedicated to the seminary students and other evangelical Christians of Colombia who have for sixteen years taught me, in spite of the injustice and persecution they have suffered, what Jesus meant when He said, "If you abide in My word, then you are truly disciples of Mine; and you shall know the truth, and the truth shall make you free."

Acknowledgments

I am deeply grateful to OMS International and especially to former Vice President David Graffenberger, who greatly encouraged me to take the time necessary to complete this book. I also wish to thank Karen Runtas, who typed the final draft, and Dr. Allan Coppedge of The Barnabas Foundation, who allowed that use of her secretarial services. I am also thankful to all of those who read the text and made helpful comments: Dr. Theo Donner and Prof. David Cosby of the Biblical Seminary of Colombia; Rev. Robert Wood of OMS International; Edward Knippers, a Christian artist; Dr. James V. Heidinger II of the Good News movement; and Dr. John Oswalt of Trinity Evangelical Divinity School. Above all, I am grateful to my wife, Sharyn White Hundley, who read every word, gave me excellent advice and encouraged me to keep at the work until it was done. Without her constant backing I could never have finished it. I also wish to express my appreciation to the staff of the Asbury Theological Seminary Library for their help in my research, especially David Bundy, John Seery and Eunice Weldon. Finally, I am very grateful to my colleagues on the faculty of the Biblical Seminary of Colombia (Jaime Ortiz Hurtado, Theo Donner, Mark Wittig, Hugo Velez, Jorge Gutierrez and David Cosby) who took many of my academic and administrative assignments upon themselves because they believed that this book "had to be written." May God be glorified!

Introduction

Liberation Theology is quickly becoming one of the most influential and controversial theological movements in the world. Less than 25 years since its birth it has already made its presence known on every continent. When I first began my study of Liberation Theology I thought it might be just another fad that would soon disappear like the "death-of-God" theology and so many others. Such was not the case. If anything, the Liberation Theology movement has expanded tremendously in the past 10 years, converting seminaries, denominations and individual Christians all over the world to its secularized version of the gospel. It is undoubtedly the fastest-growing theological movement in the world today.

My own interest in this theology began in 1970 when my wife and I first arrived in Colombia as missionaries. We were immediately confronted with the total saturation of the Colombian youth culture by the principles of revolutionary Marxism. Soon we began to hear about a new theology that combined elements of Marxism with Christianity to create a new faith that promoted violent revolution and the establishment of a socialist society. When I first heard about this I thought it was impossible that anyone could think that Christianity and Marxism could ever be combined, but I soon found that proponents of this theology were serious about doing just that. After facing a number of seminary students who came to me with questions I did not know how to answer, I decided I needed to do an in-depth study of this theology. That desire finally took us to England's Cambridge University in the fall of 1978, where I began nearly three years of post-graduate study. I spent eight hours a day, five days a week doing nothing but reading the works of the major Latin American liberation theologians, mostly in the original Spanish versions. I came away from that experience with a greater appreciation for these theologians and what they are trying to do but at the same time with a much deeper rejection of the anti-biblical root of their theology.

Having lived in Latin America since 1970, I understand why there is such a burning desire among Christians on that continent to find some way to wed their faith to a system which can enable them to participate in the revolution. I have seen children succumbing to the slow death of malnutrition, people dying in the streets for lack of adequate health care and innocent victims suffering from unspeakable horrors undergone at the hands of military torturers. So I too have felt the simmering rage that most Latin Americans feel against a system which is patently unjust, thoroughly corrupt and inhumanly cruel.

Something must be done about all of this. These injustices must not be permitted to go on. We must not see these crimes against humanity and then close our eyes and "pass by on the other side" like the indifferent men in Jesus' parable of the compassionate Samaritan. We must feel the hurt of the Third World if we are ever to understand the theology born from that hurt.

I have come to deeply respect the motives of most of the Latin American liberation theologians I have studied. For the most part they are sincere men who deeply feel the agony of their people and want to do something about it. Although some of them have not always been honest about their political persuasions, the vast majority of liberation theologians are transparent about their social, political and ideological commitments.

And so out of these attitudes of basic respect and critical analysis this book is written. I have chosen to write not as an armchair theorist sitting comfortably in the United States pontificating about the faults of exuberant Latin American theologians, but as one who lives among them, seeing what they see and hurting over the things that hurt them. I do this so that fellow Christians around the world can see this theology for what it is and judge it accordingly.

Contents

CHAPTER 1

Are There Many Liberation Theologies?

One of the most difficult problems to face in understanding the Liberation Theology movement is determining how many kinds of Liberation Theology there really are. This book will deal with the basic form—radical Latin American Liberation Theology, but many other derived varieties have been born from this radical original. In South Africa, for example, Black African Liberation Theology has been promoted by John Mbiti, Desmond Tutu and other black leaders as an expression of the black population's desire to escape apartheid's racial oppression. At the same time in the United States, James Cone and others have developed a uniquely black American application of these principles called Black Liberation Theology. Although Cone has tried to place his theological development prior to that of the Latin American liberationists, his dates are confused. He only began to use the basic concepts of Liberation Theology several years after they had been explained in print by Latin American liberationists (see his *My Soul Looks Back,* pp. 103-104).

Feminist Liberation Theology also has its roots in the Latin American movement, applying the categories of oppression and exploitation to the subjugation of women in modern society. It is important to note that although Latin American, African and some black American radical liberationists advocate revolution as the only solution to the problems they face, most of the feminists have adopted the rhetoric of Liberation Theology but do not espouse the use of violence.

Unfortunately many Christian circles have attempted to convert Liberation Theology into what liberationist Jose Miguez Bonino calls a "theological consumer product" by making it more palatable to Western theological tastes. The radical Liberation Theology of Latin America has been tamed, domesticated into a mere caricature of itself. Latin American theologians such as Mortimer Arias, Orlando Costas and Helder Camara have been presented as representative liberationists, and the essence of their message has been described as "a concern for the poor" within the limits of traditional Christianity. We must emphatically insist that, from the perspective of the true nature of radical Liberation Theology and the definition the liberationists have given their own theological "revolution," neither Arias, Costas nor Camara are true liberation theologians. Arias is a fairly conservative Methodist who believes that evangelism is the central task of the Church; Costas is a Baptist converted in a Billy Graham crusade who has attacked Liberation Theology for its universalism and reduction of the gospel to political action; and Camara is a pacifist Roman Catholic bishop who is doing his best in Brazil to promote peaceful social action as the only way to avoid the insurrection and repression that could launch a blood bath in his country.

By considering these men to be representative liberation theologians, many Western Christians have been lulled into the conclusion that Liberation Theology is nothing more than traditional Christianity with the addition of deep concern for the poor from the Latin American perspective. This is not the case at all. True

Liberation Theology is not merely ardent social concern wedded to orthodox Christian beliefs: it is a theological and doctrinal revolution that stands in opposition to the very foundations of traditional Christian doctrine. It is a whole new way of looking at the Christian faith that challenges all past ways of being Christian.

Many of the liberationists are very displeased about the "domesticating" process that is taking place in the West regarding this theology. Others however have chosen the route of soft-pedaling their more radical positions when they face Western Christians, while revealing their true convictions when they communicate with their own Latin audiences. One of the advantages of having spoken Spanish from childhood and having spent so many years living in Latin America is being privy to the full gamut of pronouncements of the liberationists, both in their more guarded English presentations as well as in their more candid Spanish and Portuguese ones. For that reason, one of the purposes of this book is to allow the liberationists to "speak for themselves," revealing the truly radical nature of their theological revolution. In this sense, although there are many liberation theologies, we will be looking at only one of them, radical Latin American Liberation Theology. But it is the most fundamental, the most radical and, at the same time, the most authentic of all of them.

CHAPTER 2

How Was Liberation Theology Born?

Many people believe that Liberation Theology is a Roman Catholic movement that began at the CELAM II (Second General Council of the Latin American Episcopate) conference in Medellin, Colombia, in 1968.[1] Such is not the case. Nine years before the Roman Catholic Latin American bishops met in Medellin a movement called "ISAL"[2] was born among Protestant Latin American theologians to promote the study of Christian social responsibility. ISAL, which stands for "Iglesia y Sociedad en America Latina" (Church and Society in Latin America), was founded under the auspices of the World Council of Churches and was heavily influenced by that organization.

As these Latin American Protestants began to reflect on how to solve the social problems of Latin America, they soon concluded that the Bible offers little or no help for such a task. They saw the Bible as self-contradictory and pre-scientific in its social principles and other-worldly in its interests, and they adopted the liberal view that Jesus' teaching was for the "end times" and therefore not applicable to modern Christian living in any direct way. This view of the inability of the Scriptures to provide specific and authoritative guidelines for

Christian social action caused them to seek some other norm for Christian conduct in the face of Latin American suffering. This rejection of the Scriptures' claim to speak on social as well as personal and spiritual issues became the foundation of the radical Liberation Theology movement. Dismissing the possibility of finding scriptural answers to their questions regarding Christian conduct in oppressive societies, the ISAL theologians were forced to launch into a prolonged debate about which social change theory they should accept.

For the next few years the ISAL official magazine, *Cristianismo y Sociedad* (Christianity and Society), ran a long series of articles in which the movement's leaders debated how they could help alleviate the misery and suffering in Latin American life. Some proposed "reform" as the best way to solve social problems, believing that Latin America could be changed through better laws, better health facilities, better education and a more just economic distribution. Others, however, felt there was no hope in reform because of the closed, oppressive social structures of Latin America which, they believed, made effective change for the poor impossible. They insisted on a revolutionary solution—overthrowing the present unjust regimes and establishing a just social order. In the course of the debate the reformists pointed out the violent nature of revolution and concluded that Christians should not participate in that kind of destruction and killing regardless of good results. On the other hand, the revolutionists pointed out that Christian love for the poor and oppressed could only be lived concretely through the destruction of unjust structures and the establishment of a socialist society in which there would be no more poverty and oppression.

Two important influences tipped the scales in ISAL from reform to revolution: the success of the Cuban Revolution and the new theological concepts advocated by Richard Shaull, who introduced the thinking of Dietrich Bonhoeffer and Paul Lehmann. The Cuban Revolution of 1959 has been called "the most decisive event in modern Latin American history" by Orlando Costas, who believes that it has become the model for all Latin American nations in their struggle for political change. The relative success of the Cuban Revolution demonstrated to Latin Americans that the United States would tolerate a Marxist government in Latin America, Christianity could coexist with Marxism and Marxist revolution could possibly be seen as the most effective means for expressing Christian love for the poor and exploited. The ISAL leaders began making regular trips to Cuba after the revolution, returning with glowing accounts of the "new paradise" being constructed there. Many of the ISAL members, who questioned whether revolution was practical for Latin America in the face of United States dominance on the continent, saw the triumph of Marxist revolution in Cuba as an affirmative answer to their questions.

Richard Shaull arrived in Colombia as a Presbyterian missionary in 1942. He served there until 1951, then moved to Brazil where he taught in the Presbyterian Seminary in Campinas. Through his association with young people in the Student Christian Movement[3] of Latin America who were actively committed to revolution, Shaull became more and more radical in his political and theological views. He came to see revolution as the only hope for Latin America and dedicated a great deal of his efforts to convincing the ISAL theologians to make the same commitment. Shaull tried to prove that the God of the Bible is a God of liberation and that He is always on the side of the liberators against the oppressors.

Shaull brought the writings of Dietrich Bonhoeffer to Latin America in 1952, introducing many Protestant theologians to the thinking of the man who loved peace but was imprisoned for taking part in a plot to assassinate Adolph Hitler. Julio de Santa Ana, one of the early leaders of ISAL, has explained that many ISAL members found that they could agree with Bonhoeffer's statement that Christians today must "live in the world as if God did not exist"—they must solve their own problems and work for the betterment of humanity without expecting God to intervene. The ISAL leaders also accepted Bonhoeffer's argument for the temporary use of violence by Christians to halt evil that cannot be stopped any other way. Shaull's translation of parts of Bonhoeffer's *Letters and Papers from Prison*[4] *convinced many in the ISAL movement not only that they could* participate in violent revolution, but also that as Christians they *must* do so in order to be true to the gospel.

In 1961 Shaull brought his mentor, Paul Lehmann, to Latin America for a tour of Brazil and Argentina. Lehmann lectured to seminary students, professors and student leaders about the possibility that God was using the Marxist revolutionary movement to humanize[5] Latin America and that the Church should join Him in that project. Lehmann's lectures made a tremendous impact on many Latin American Protestant leaders, including many in ISAL. Since Lehmann identified "humanization" (working to make human life human) as the essence of both Christian faith and Marxist dogma, he could encourage the union of Christianity and Marxism by asserting that they share the same final goal for humanity. This was to become one of the fundamental arguments of radical Liberation Theology in the future.

In 1964 Rubem Alves, a former disciple of Richard Shaull in the seminary in Brazil, wrote a watershed article in *Cristianismo y Sociedad* which sealed the revolutionary option of ISAL.[6] Although ISAL still continued to publish a small number of non-revolutionary articles, the major direction of the magazine from 1964 turned toward a "clear revolutionary and socialist option," according to liberationist ISAL leader Jose Miguez Bonino.

The major points of Alves' article are crucially important for a clear understanding of radical Liberation Theology's beginnings. His article, "Injusticia y rebelion" ("Injustice and Rebellion"), affirms that: (1) the underdeveloped nations of the Third World are maintained in economic dependency by the rich nations who

derive their wealth from exploiting the poorer nations;
(2) the hidden problem of Latin America which gener-
ates its suffering is "class struggle" between the poor
proletariat and the rich capitalists; (3) the essence of
both Christianity and Marxism is humanization, therefore, Christians and Marxists can unite to reach their
common goal; (4) God does not reveal Himself in the
Scriptures but in events of modern history such as the
search for human liberation; (5) God is at work in the
Marxist revolutionary movement to bring His kingdom
to Latin America; and (6) the Church should join the
Marxists to bring about the revolution. These six points
are still the basic tenets of radical Liberation Theology.

By 1965 (three years before the CELAM II meetings in
Medellin) the ISAL magazine had outlined the major
doctrines of what Rubem Alves had christened the
"theology of liberation." ISAL leaders affirmed that
God is present in the Marxist revolutionary movement
to bring His kingdom to Latin America and that the
Church should join Him and participate in the revolution. They concluded that the Marxist analysis of the
social problems of Latin America, based on the theories
of class struggle and the evils of private property, was
correct and that the only way to solve those problems
was through a violent revolution and the establishment
of a socialist society in Latin America. They were convinced that they would be able to create a new form of
Marxist socialism capable of escaping the failures of
international communism. In brief, they had come to
believe that God was behind the revolution to bring His
kingdom to Latin America in the form of Marxist socialism, purged from its atheistic tendencies.[7]

ISAL was the nest in which radical Liberation Theology was born. It was nurtured and encouraged by
Richard Shaull, Paul Lehmann and the writings of Dietrich Bonhoeffer, but the distinction of writing its first
Latin American presentation belongs to Rubem Alves,
who outlined the main points of this theology in his
article, "Injusticia y rebelion," in 1964. There was a
great deal of cross-fertilization between Protestant and

Roman Catholic theologians during the following four years (especially between Alves and Gustavo Gutierrez) which finally resulted in the theological bombshell that was exploded at the CELAM II conferences in Medellin in 1968. There many Latin American Roman Catholic theologians publicly committed themselves to the newly-christened "Theology of Liberation." Although many of those same theologians have now backed down on their commitment to radical Liberation Theology in light of Vatican opposition, support for this theological revolution in the Roman Catholic Latin American Church has mushroomed. Similar growth has been seen in many sectors of the Protestant Church in Latin America. The embryonic theology that began among a small group of Latin American Protestant theologians has now touched every continent with its call to "put down your Bibles, take up your rifles and join the revolution."

Chapter 2, Notes
_____

1. CELAM stands for "Consejo General del Episcopado Latinoamericano" (General Council of the Latin American Episcopate). This Council of Latin American bishops was founded in 1955 to study the specific problems of Latin America. The second meeting of the Council in 1968 was surrounded by serious tensions within the Latin American Roman Catholic Church. Although the purpose of that second meeting was to apply the principles of Vatican II (1965) to Latin America, there was a great deal of controversy among the bishops as to how that should be done.
    Some bishops advocated radical social action, while others resisted revolution and were quick to label their more radical colleagues as communists. The final document of CELAM II denounced both capitalism and Marxism and called for liberation from all oppression. Although the atheistic materialism of Marxism was criticized, "capitalistic imperialism" received far greater blame for the suffering of Latin America. The "Theology of Liberation" was presented as a better option, both biblically and politically, than the theologies of development/reform which it replaced.
2. ISAL came into existence as the result of the founding of a regional secretariat for Latin America by the World Council of Churches in 1959. The WCC secretary immediately published a bulletin bearing the "ISAL" name and convened a Latin American Consultation on Church and Society for 1961. ISAL was born out of that Consultation in 1962. Although ISAL never represented a large

number of Protestant Christians, it exercised a disproportionate influence on Latin American Christianity until it was expelled from Chile as a subversive organization by the government in 1973. The publications of ISAL have continued even after its executive committee officially dissolved the organization in 1974. *Cristianismo y Sociedad* is still being produced in a persistent effort to promote the ISAL liberationist position.

3. The Student Christian Movement was an international network of students committed to the Christian faith. Although the SCM had strong evangelical beginnings, many of the Latin American SCM groups began a process of increasing radicalization in 1956. By 1964 many of the national SCM committees had openly declared their commitment to radical social change through Marxist revolution.

4. *Letters and Papers from Prison* was the compilation of various letters, poems, prayers, sermons and thoughts written by Dietrich Bonhoeffer during his imprisonment by the Nazis for participating in a plot to kill Hitler. They were obviously not intended by Bonhoeffer to be a systematic presentation of Christian truth, and many of them may be little more than the thinking out loud of a Christian caught in very difficult personal circumstances. Nevertheless these writings have been used heavily by the liberationists in the formulation of their theological positions. Many Bonhoeffer experts have complained that the liberation theologians have grossly misinterpreted Bonhoeffer's intentions.

5. "Humanization" is one of those theological catchwords which has become very popular in the last few decades. It literally means "to make human," but it is so vague that it can be filled up with almost any content its user desires. In Liberation Theology it is used to speak of raising people up out of their sub-human state of oppression, ignorance and misery and restoring their human dignity and a decent level of economic and social existence. Lehmann suggested during his South American tour that the foundation of true cooperation between Christians and Marxists is the fact that both "share a passion for the humanization of man." However what is "human" for the Christian, we would insist, is far different from that which is "human" for the Marxist, since the Christian's vision of what God intended man to be comes from the Scriptures. That view is a far cry from the goals for man presented in the writings of Karl Marx.

6. Rubem Alves, "Injusticia y rebelion," *Cristianismo y Sociedad* No. 6 (1964), pp. 40-53.

7. See, for example, *Cristianismo y Sociedad* No. 2 (1963), pp. 1-3; No. 3 (1963), pp. 30-42; No. 6 (1964), pp. 1-2, 31-39, 40-53; No. 7 (1965), pp. 6-15, 26-35, 49-52, 53-60; No. 8 (1965), pp. 30-52, 62-69, 70-90, 91-95.

CHAPTER 3

How Do Liberation Theologians Do Theology?

The most important radical liberation theologians in Latin America are Gustavo Gutierrez, Jose Miguez Bonino, Rubem Alves, Leonardo Boff, Jose Severino Croatto, Jose Porfirio Miranda, Hugo Assmann and Juan Luis Segundo. These men have written the greatest number of books and articles from the perspective of Liberation Theology, and they are the leaders of the movement. Although they share many concepts, they are all individuals with unique contributions to the growth and development of radical Liberation Theology. In this chapter we will consider in some detail the Liberation Theology of Gutierrez, Alves and Miguez as representative of the entire group and as major contributors to the formation of radical Liberation Theology.

GUSTAVO GUTIERREZ: Gustavo Gutierrez is a Roman Catholic priest from Peru. He was born in Lima in 1928 and studied psychiatry and philosophy in the San Marcos and Catholic Universities of Lima where he was very active in socialist political groups among students.[1] Gutierrez met Camilo Torres, the "revolutionary priest" of Colombia, while studying in Louvain, Belgium, in 1953, and they became life-long friends. Many believe that Gutierrez' theological writings are the extension of his commitment to the revolution espoused by his friend Torres, who joined the Marxist guerrilla army in 1965 and was killed in a shoot-out with the Colombian army in 1966. Gutierrez has a very good theological education and his works reflect his broad knowledge of European and North American theologians. He is active in university teaching and as an adviser to student and workers' movements in Peru. His commitment to the poor is exemplified in his simple lifestyle and personal solidarity with their lot.

The distinctive feature of Gutierrez' presentation of radical Liberation Theology is the systematic, logical way he makes his case. Some have even called him the "systematic theologian of Liberation Theology" because of his orderly, reasoned classic work, *A Theology of Liberation: Perspectives.* He began working on this basic argument in 1968 and finally published the finished volume in 1971. Gutierrez' basic argument is that Christians must cease doing theology on the basis of interpreting the Scriptures and begin seeing theology as "critical reflection on liberating praxis."[2] This phrase is so crucial to Gutierrez' theology that it merits a word-by-word analysis. "Liberating praxis" for Gutierrez is active participation in the revolutionary movement to establish a socialist society in Latin America.[3] He believes that right faith must begin from the perspective of a Christian already actively involved in revolution. Gutierrez argues strongly against any attempt to do theology based on biblical interpretation as a first step.[4] Although he realizes fully that traditional Christian theology has been founded on the interpretation of Scripture and the application of that interpretation to contemporary life, he argues for a theological revolution, a "new way of doing theology," which begins, not with the Word of God, but with liberating praxis as its foundation.[5]

Gutierrez stresses the "critical" nature of his reflection because he believes that Christians must be made aware that not all "praxis" is truly liberating.[6] He believes that Christians have a unique contribution to make to the revolution once they are committed to it. They can make sure that the liberating praxis is neither worshipped nor made an absolute.[7] Theology functions within a prior commitment to revolution to sharpen and refine that commitment.[8] Perhaps the following diagram can illustrate this idea graphically:

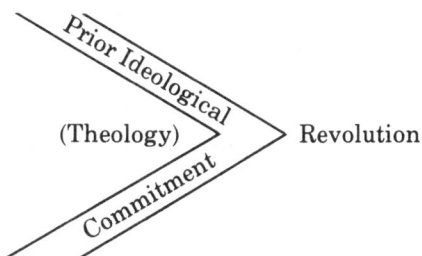

Prior Ideological

(Theology)   Revolution

Commitment

In this diagram we can see the central, unique element of Gutierrez' presentation of radical Liberation Theology: Theology is placed within the context of a prior commitment to liberating praxis for revolution. As Gutierrez has said, theology is not meant to "justify that commitment" but to be the "fruit of a faith lived and thought out from within the questions presented by the liberating praxis in order to make a more creative insertion in it."[9] Theology, in this view, has become the handmaiden of revolutionary commitment, enhancing and strengthening it in order to make it more effective.

What is the evangelical analysis of this foundational doctrine in Gutierrez' Liberation Theology?

1. *The best evangelical theologians are aware that none of us do theology purely from our study of the Scriptures.*[10] All interpreters of God's Word come with certain concepts, a definite culture and a specific ideological position that makes our interpretation less than purely objective. We do not dispute

Rudolph Bultmann's claim that there is no "presuppositionless exegesis," but we refuse to accept the conclusion that since totally objective interpretation is impossible, the Christian theologian should give up that ideal and devote himself to biblical interpretation filtered through his own philosophical and ideological positions. Just because we can't be perfectly objective does not mean that we should become totally subjective in our interpretation of scripture. The problem with Gutierrez is that in the most important decision he has ever made as a Christian—that of committing himself to revolution—his "new way of doing theology" has cut him off from the determining influence of the Word of God. Everything in his theology flows from his commitment to revolution, yet in that all-important commitment he will not allow the Scriptures to have the last word. That is totally unacceptable to evangelicals.

2. *Although evangelicals realize that it is difficult to rid ourselves of political, cultural and ideological biases as we come to Scripture, we honestly seek to do so as much as possible.* Perhaps the following three diagrams will illustrate this point:

Fundamen- talist View	Liberal/Neo- Evangelical View	Evangelical View

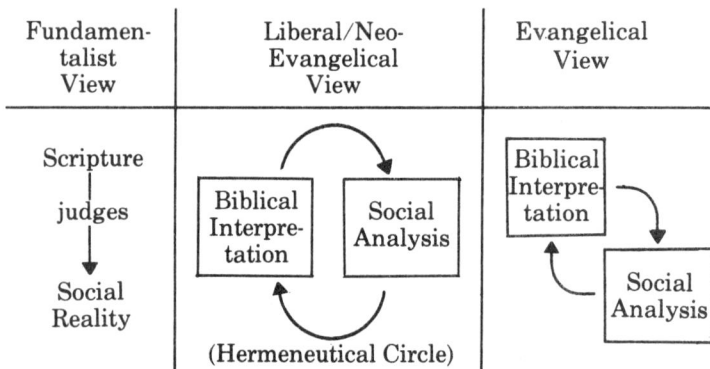

(Hermeneutical Circle)

The first diagram represents the fundamentalist position which pretends to judge social reality solely on the basis of Scripture. This position is naive because it does not take into account the way our previous understanding of politics, economics and social order affect our interpretation of the Scriptures. We do not come to the Word with empty heads but with all kinds of notions about justice, democracy, revolution, law, order, race, poverty, wealth, international trade, morality and many other subjects. Some of those concepts have been formed on biblical bases, but others have not. We must become aware of these preconceptions if we are to expose them to the authoritative light of Scripture and allow God to change them when they are not in harmony with His revealed will.

In the second diagram we see the "hermeneutical circle." In it, biblical interpretation and social analysis are placed in a circle of mutual influence and interdependence. In the hermeneutical circle neither has priority. Each influences the other in an equal way: a person's analysis of social reality determines his/her interpretation of Scripture and his/her biblical interpretation determine his/her social analysis. This is the view of liberalism, neo-evangelicalism and the New Hermeneutic.[11]

The third diagram illustrates the evangelical view. This position takes into account the influence of social analysis on biblical interpretation and, at the same time, makes clear that the priority in this relationship is to be placed on biblical interpretation, not social analysis. Although social analysis influences the kinds of questions we ask the biblical text, the truths discovered in Scripture have the "last word" in any discussion with social analysis. Thus if a person's social analysis teaches that humanity's central problem is economic and that this basic problem can be solved by a new economic order, the interpreter's understanding of biblical truth corrects that idea and brings it under the authority of God's Word. He/she would reject the idea whether the new economic order recommended is socialism or the free enterprise system.

3. *Much of Gutierrez' insistence on not beginning theology in submission to the authority of the*

Word of God seems to stem from his own recognition that the Bible would not justify the kind of violent, revolutionary praxis he espouses.[12] It is amazing to see the lengths to which many modern theologians will go to undermine the authority of God's Word if it either prohibits something they want to do or commands something they don't want to do. Sadly, it seems that much of today's theology, including Gutierrez' radical Liberation Theology, is merely an attempt to assert the same kind of autonomy from and defiance of God's authority that we see in the fall of Adam and Eve in Genesis 3. Although all generalizations can be oversimplified, it appears that much of modern theology involves attempting to find intellectual substitutes for a personal, loving relationship with God in Christ and a life of obedient submission to His Word. As evangelicals we have a tremendous responsibility to proclaim the need of every person (and this includes modern theologians) to find spiritual fulfillment in a relationship with God in Jesus Christ that is both loving and obedient. As we do, we need to confess humbly that even much of modern evangelicalism is long on the "personal" side of the relationship and short on the "obedient" side.

RUBEM ALVES: Chronologically, the very first Latin American to publish a declaration of the basic tenets of radical Liberation Theology was the Brazilian (former) Presbyterian theologian, Rubem Alves.[13] Alves became a Christian through the preaching he heard in an evangelical Presbyterian Church in Brazil. He longed to prepare himself to become "the Billy Graham of Brazil," so he attended the Presbyterian Seminary of Brazil. Instead of having his faith strengthened and matured, he came into contact with American missionary Richard Shaull who destroyed Alves' evangelical faith, awakened him to the suffering of the poor and influenced him towards radical political activism.[14] In recalling that experience, Alves has said that for him, "God died . . . His name ceased to be a symbol of freedom and love. And we felt that maybe we were alone before the task of rebuilding the world and that our strength was the only power available in the accomplishment of this task."[15] Alves soon had to face the question, "If God is not active today in any supernatural way, was He in the days described in the Bible?" Alves' answer was "no." He came to believe that the Bible was the result of the imposition of "God-language" by the community of faith on events that were purely natural.[16] For example, Alves suggested that the Exodus event was really just a violent uprising by a group of Semitic slaves who, when they recorded what happened centuries later, wrote the story as if God had done it, using plagues and miracles to make it sound more important.[17]

With their anti-supernatural view of Christianity, Alves and his friends launched themselves into the Brazilian revolutionary movement with great hopes for man's ability to solve his own problems, but the revolution was destroyed by the Brazilian military. Looking back, Alves concluded that many of the Marxist revolutionaries were as anti-human as the capitalist exploiters and that "it is as difficult to believe that anti-human factors will produce a human result as it is to believe in the God of traditional theology."[18] Having rejected his former evangelical faith and his new liberationist one, Alves began to proclaim a "Theology of Captivity" in which he urged Latin Americans to accept the fact that they might never see their liberation but that their grandchildren might.[19]

In a 1984 interview in Brazil, this author asked Alves what he considered himself to be since he was no longer evangelical or liberationist. His answer was, "I am a mystic." He now spends much of his time writing poems and meditating on the beauty of nature, Gandhi and magic. When asked what he thought of modern liberationists, he responded, "They are fascists!"

Alves' pilgrimage from evangelical believer to liberationist to mystic indicates the destiny of those who deny God's action in history and the authority of His Word, placing their hopes in human efforts. The scriptural warning, "Cursed is the man who trusts in mankind

and makes flesh his strength, and whose heart turns
away from the Lord" (Jeremiah 17:5), is still valid today.
Many liberation theologians have not been as honest as
Alves in denouncing the evils of some Marxist revolutionaries who rival corrupt capitalists in their hunger
for power and position.
Alves finally rejected Marxism and its illusory prom-
ises because he saw it as "anti-human" since it makes
people a means to an end and makes economics the final
criterion for judging the quality of life.[20] His disillu-
sionment with the revolutionary process and subse-
quent rejection of Liberation Theology for its naive view
of human nature and social change should serve as a
warning to any who would, in the name of Christian
truth, substitute the authority of Marxist revolutionary
theory for the norm of Scripture.

JOSE MIGUEZ BONINO: The theological journey of
Jose Miguez Bonino serves as a representative portrait
of the liberationist commitment of many Protestant
theologians in Latin America today. Miguez, who was
born in Argentina in 1924, has been called "the out-
standing Protestant contributor to all of Latin American theology."[21] He began as a conservative evangelical
scholar concerned about the best way to evangelize the
Roman Catholic Church in Latin America.[22] Then,
influenced by his studies at Emory University and
Union Theological Seminary, he adopted a more neo-
orthodox view of the Bible. In this view the "Word of
God" is not seen as the Scriptures themselves but as
"the encounter of Jesus Christ with the human soul,
that takes place when the Church proclaims Christ
faithfully, as the Scriptures give testimony of him."[23] In
this period Miguez addressed himself to the social
responsibility of the Church, stating that the Bible gives
no satisfactory norm for Christian social action because
it offers no universal principles for conduct.[24] In 1969
Miguez was still critical of Alves and other Protestant
liberation theologians who, he felt, were in danger of
reducing the gospel to politics, losing the Church's spe-

cifically Christian character by identifying it with all groups struggling for liberation, placing ideological commitment as the center of Christian faith rather than Jesus Christ and maintaining dependence on the theologies of Europe and North America on which their Liberation Theology was based.[25] At the same time he was becoming more and more aware that, as a Latin American, he had to do something to help stop the suffering of his poverty-stricken compatriots.

In 1971 and 1972 Miguez changed his critical position regarding radical Liberation Theology, presumably under the influence of the meetings of the ISAL theologians in Peru and the Christians for Socialism Encounter in Santiago, Chile. By 1972 he had come to openly espouse a "strategic alliance" between Christians and Marxists in order to carry out their common project for the liberation of Latin America.[26]

One of Miguez' primary contributions to the Liberation Theology debate has been his ability to articulate clearly and convincingly the basic tenets of this theological revolution, especially the place of praxis in theology, the relationship between Christians and Marxists, the use of violence for revolution and the marks of Christian love from a liberationist perspective. He has become the most recognized and eloquent voice for radical Liberation Theology in most parts of the world. His extensive travels and voluminous writings have given his ideas wide exposure and placed him in a unique position to champion Liberation Theology to the Western world.

One of the most forceful elements of Miguez' theology is his opposition to any form of "idealistic Western theology" in which general principles are drawn from studying the biblical text and then applied to specific situations in daily life.[27] He frequently and systematically denounces this way of doing theology as totally inadequate because it violates the nature of the biblical text and the demands of complex modern society.[28] Miguez insists that theology must be born out of the action of committed Christians working for the liberation of mankind, not out of ideas taken from a "sacred text."[29] His arguments seem convincing until you begin to consider the alternative to thought before action—action without thought! It is impossible to act without thinking first. It is impossible to choose a course of action ("praxis") without some guiding principles on which that choice is made. All action is based on previously thought-out concepts, even Miguez' commitment to revolutionary praxis. He reveals this in his book, *Doing Theology in a Revolutionary Situation,* where he is forced to admit that he too bases his action on certain "constancies or (with all necessary caveats) laws" (p. 97). "Caveat" is a Latin word meaning "beware" and gives the idea of warning. Miguez is obviously aware that he is on dangerous ground when he violates his own strong arguments and suggests that the Christian's action in history should be based on certain "constancies" or "laws." He goes on to state that the "laws" that Christians should use to guide their actions are taken from Marxism.[30] In the same work, Miguez identifies Marxism as "the unavoidable historical mediation of Christian obedience" and "a scientific, verifiable and efficacious way to articulate love historically."[31] It is not that Miguez has actually broken the pattern of evangelical theology in drawing general principles and then applying them to life; rather, he has substituted Marxism for the Scriptures as the source of the principles he chooses to apply. Sadly, he has been unable to escape the "ideologization" of the gospel that he once eloquently warned against in which Liberation Theology:

> ... appears as the hopeless prisoner of a hermeneutical circle, the spell of which it cannot break. The text of Scripture and tradition is forced into the Procrustean bed of ideology, and the theologian who has fallen prey of this procedure is forever condemned to listen only to the echo of his own ideology. There is no redemption for this theology, because it has muzzled the Word of God in its transcendence and freedom.[32]

Gustavo Gutierrez, Rubem Alves and Jose Miguez

Bonino are three of the most important Latin American liberation theologians. They point out the strengths and the weaknesses of this theology which, in its honest attempt to respond to the misery of a continent, has slipped away from the mooring of God's Word and floats adrift in a sea of ideological confusion.

Chapter 3, Notes

1. Derek Winter, *Hope in Captivity* (London: Epworth Press, 1977), p. 27.
2. Gutierrez, *Teologia de la liberacion: perspectivas* (Salamanca: Sigueme, 1980), p. 40.
3. *Ibid.*, pp. 126-127, 129-130; and Gutierrez, "Apuntes para una teologia para la liberacion," *Cristianismo y Sociedad* 24/25 (1970), pp. 10-11.
4. Gutierrez, "Movimientos de liberacion y teologia," *Concilium* 93 (1974), p. 450.
5. "Entrevista con Gustavo Gutierrez," in *Nuevo Mundo* 66 (1975), p. 325; and Gutierrez, *Teologia de la liberacion: perspectivas,* pp. 40-41.
6. Gutierrez, *Teologia de la liberacion: perspectivas,* p. 118; and Gutierrez, "Apuntes para una teologia para la liberacion," pp. 10-11.
7. Gutierrez, *Teologia de la liberacion: perspectivas,* p. 36.
8. Gutierrez, "Movimientos de liberacion y teologia," p. 451.
9. *Ibid.*
10. See, for example, Graham N. Stanton, "Presuppositions in New Testament Criticism," in I. Howard Marshall (ed.), *New Testament Interpretation* (Grand Rapids: Eerdmans, 1977), pp. 60-71; Donald Guthrie, *New Testament Theology* (Downers Grove: Inter-Varsity, 1981), pp. 42-47, 953-982; and F. F. Bruce, "The History of New Testament Study," in Marshall (ed.), *New Testament Interpretation,* pp. 51-53.
11. See, for example, Anthony C. Thiselton, *The Two Horizons* (Grand Rapids: Eerdmans, 1980), pp. 103-114; Walter C. Kaiser, Jr., *Toward an Exegetical Theology* (Grand Rapids: Baker Book House, 1981), pp. 23-36; D. A. Carson, "A Sketch of the Factors Determining Current Hermeneutical Debate in Cross-Cultural Contexts," (in D. A. Carson (ed.), *Biblical Interpretation and the Church* (NY: Thomas Nelson, 1984), pp. 12-15; and Anthony C. Thiselton, "The New Hermeneutic," in Marshall (ed.), *New Testament Interpretation,* pp. 312-318.
12. Gutierrez, "Movimentos de liberacion y teologia," pp. 449-453; Gutierrez, "Apuntes para una teologia para la liberacion," pp. 8-11; and Gutierrez, *Teologia de la liberacion: perspectivas,* p. 78.
13. See the discussion of Alves' contribution to the birth of Liberation Theology above in Chapter Two. His *Cristianismo y Sociedad*

article in 1964 antedates the birthdate set for Liberation Theology, by Andrew Kirk (see his *Liberation Theology,* p. 23); Orlando Costas (see his *Theology of the Crossroads in Contemporary Latin America,* pp. 73-74); and Rosino Gibellini (see his *Frontiers of Theology in Latin America,* p. ix).

14.   Alan Preston Neely, "Protestant Antecedents of the Theology of Liberation," doctoral dissertation, American University, 1977, p. 278; Derek Winter, *Hope in Captivity,* pp. 58-59; and from a personal conversation with Dr. Jaime Ortiz Hurtado, rector of the Seminario Biblico de Colombia, who studied with Alves in Brazil.

15.   Alves, "Confessions: On Theology and Life," *Union Seminary Quarterly Review* XXIX:3/4 (1974), p. 184.

16.   Alves, "Theses for a Reconstruction of Theology," *Documents—IDOC* (October 31, 1970), p. 14.

17.   *Ibid.*; Alves, "El pueblo de Dios y la busqueda de una nueva ordenacion social," in Gustavo Gutierrez and others, *Religion, instrumento de liberacion?* (Barcelona: Marova y Fontanella, 1973), pp. 133-146; and Alves, *A Theology of Human Hope* (Washington: Corpus, 1969), pp. 135-136.

18.   Alves, "Marxism as the Guarantee of Faith," *Worldview* (March, 1973), p. 17.

19.   Alves, *Tomorrow's Child: Imagination, Creativity and the Rebirth of Culture* (London: SCM Press, 1972), pp. 188-204.

20.   Alves, "Marxism as the Guarantee of Faith," pp. 15-17.

21.   Neely, "Protestant Antecedents," p. 312.

22.   Miguez, "Nuestro Mensaje," in *Cristo, la Esperanza para America Latina* (Lima: II Conferencia Evangelica Latinoamericana, 1961), p. 87.

23.   Miguez, "Escritura y tradicion: un antiguo problema en una nueva perspectiva," *Cuadernos Teologicos* 34 (1960), p. 104. (This statement reflects the views of Karl Barth and Emil Brunner).

24.   Miguez, "Fundamento biblico de la responsabilidad de la iglesia en la sociedad," *Cuadernos Teologicos* 40 (1961), pp. 231-233.

25.   Miguez, "El Camino del Teologo Protestante Latinoamericano," *Cuadernos de Marcha* 29 (September, 1969), pp. 64-66.

26.   Miguez, "Partidismo o Solidaridad?," *Cristianismo y Sociedad* 33/34 (1972), pp. 96-98.

27.   Miguez, "The Struggle of the Poor and the Church," *Ecumenical Review* XXVII:1 (January, 1975), pp. 24, 40; Miguez, *Christians and Marxists: The Mutual Challenge to Revolution* (Grand Rapids: Eerdmans, 1976), p. 30; and Miguez, *Doing Theology in a Revolutionary Situation* (Philadelphia: Fortress, 1975), p. 88.

28.   *Ibid.*

29.   Miguez, *Doing Theology in a Revolutionary Situation,* p. 88.

30.   *Ibid.,* p. 97.

31.   *Ibid.,* pp. 97-98.

32.   *Ibid.,* p. 87.

CHAPTER 4

What About The Bible?

The major issue that separates evangelical Christianity from all other forms of Christian faith is our belief in the unique, absolute and final authority of the Bible for Christian faith and practice.[1] All the other differences regarding conversion, a personal relationship with God in Christ, judgment, heaven, hell and morality are based on that one main difference—evangelicals believe that the Bible is the last word for Christians. So, in analyzing any theology, it is crucial that evangelicals carefully evaluate the view the theologians have of the Bible. This is the central issue in an evangelical evaluation of radical Liberation Theology. It is not their politics nor their economics nor even their ideological position that should be the focus of our criticism of the liberationists; it is their view of Scripture.[2] They have attempted to build a theological system in which the Word of God does not have the last word, and as evangelicals we cannot accept that position.[3]

As we have already pointed out in chapter two, rejecting the Scriptures' authority in determining Christian social action was ISAL's first step toward the birth of Liberation Theology among the Protestant theologians of that group. It is impossible to create a radical Liberation Theology unless the authority of the Bible for Christian faith and practice is first denied. Since the

Bible not only does not advocate revolution but actually prohibits it for Christians (see Romans 3:1-7 and 1 Peter 2:13-17, for example), anyone wishing to call the Christian Church to active participation in armed insurrection must first wean the Church away from its submission to the authoritative voice of God's Word.[4] In general, the Protestant liberationists do this through the use of radical biblical criticism while the Roman Catholic liberationists do it through the doctrine of open revelation, although there is a great deal of overlap between them. Radical biblical criticism tends to consider the Bible to be merely a human book written by pre-scientific religious people who invented much of what they wrote. Their writings therefore hold little or no authority for us today. The Roman Catholic doctrine of open revelation holds that the writings of the Scriptures are truly revealed by God and authoritative, but it adds that God is still revealing equally authoritative doctrines through the leaders of the Roman Catholic Church. Ultimately both groups deny the final authority of the Scriptures.

Protestants like Rubem Alves, the founder of Liberation Theology, used the most radical results of modern criticism to destroy the Bible's authority for Christians. Alves suggested that "truth" is merely "the name given by a historical community to its historical deeds which were, are and will be efficacious in the liberation of man."[5] He insisted that "revelation" is merely a way of talking about conclusions as if God had spoken them.[6] With these two concepts Alves relegated all of Scripture to sheer human invention. According to the picture he presents, the Israelites experienced some wonderful events as a community which assured their survival as a people.[7] These events were purely natural, accomplished solely by the Israelites themselves, but when they recorded them for posterity, they wanted to make them sound more important. So, they used "God-language" to describe what had happened, attributing to God what they themselves had done.[8]

If this is true for the rest of the Bible, then all of the

commandments and teachings in the Old and New Testaments are merely the religious speculations of the Israelites and the early Christian community, not inspired words from God as the Scriptures say they are.[9] Naturally then we should not be required to seek after models in these writings since we are in the same position as the authors. We must also look at the events around us and attribute the liberating acts of our history to God, according to Alves.[10] He criticizes the evangelical approach which limits special revelation to the biblical record, insisting that "the Christian attitude . . . is not the tracing of a model already given, but participation in the action of God within the concrete circumstances in which we live."[11]

As evangelicals we also believe that God is at work in the world today, but we believe that He calls us to work in accord with His revealed will in His written Word, not according to some vague notion of "what He is doing today in history." How can we know what He is doing in history today and what our response to it should be apart from the teaching of Scripture? If a capitalist tells us that God is in favor of the ruthless accumulation of wealth as proof of personal worth, we must respond with what Jesus said, "not *even* when one has an abundance does his life consist of his possessions" (Luke 12:15 - see also Luke 12:13-34; 1 Timothy 6:6-10, 17-19; Matthew 19:16-26; Colossians 3:5; James 5:1-6). We have no other answer and we need no other; that is enough. God promised the Israelites that their obedience to His Word would be their "wisdom and understanding" in the sight of the nations they met (Deuteronomy 4:6), and Jesus told His disciples that "everyone who hears these words of Mine, and acts upon them, may be compared to a wise man" (Matthew 7:24). The Christian faith is not some kind of blind leap in the dark, trying to guess at what God is doing in history and join Him in it. It is a life of obedience to God's will as He has revealed it in His inspired, supernatural Word.[12] The rejection of this foundational truth marks the tragic flaw of Alves' entire theological system.

Roman Catholic liberationist Leonardo Boff echoes many of Alves' sentiments. He begins by arguing against the idea of anything "supernatural" occurring in human history. He agrees with Alves that the supernatural is just a primitive way of speaking of events that were purely historical and natural.[13] He insists that revelation "does not fall from heaven" but "is produced in history."[14] He sees the production of the Scriptures as merely a part of the wider natural process in which all people try to interpret the meaning of life. Boff believes that as people pass through the experiences of life they ask themselves, "What does this mean? What does my life mean?" He believes that people have to answer these questions for themselves but that some try to exalt their opinions about the meaning of life by attributing them to God.[15] In this sense, for Boff the task of the Christian faith "does not reside primarily in the interpretation of the Scriptures, but in the interpretation of life."[16] Boff explains his view of "open revelation" by his rejection of the "archaeological" view of revelation, which sees revelation as "accomplished in the past and finalized with the death of the last apostle," and by affirming his own "liberal theology" (as he calls it) which declares the "permanent present time of the revelatory event."[17]

Boff's distinction is very important. Evangelical Christianity clearly rests its beliefs on what Boff calls the "archaeological view." We affirm that the revelation God gave in the Old and New Testaments is unique, final and closed. Boff sees it as ordinary, temporary and open. We live in an age when Boff's view is seen as praiseworthy, and our view is deemed thoroughly objectionable.[18] Modern secularist thought can tolerate any form of belief except the belief that there are absolute answers to life's questions.[19] Modern pluralistic society can accept witchcraft more easily than it can accept evangelical Christianity. Why? Because evangelical faith declares that God has spoken in an absolute, final way about human thought, beliefs and conduct and that the duty of every human being in the face of God's revelation is faith and submission. This is a tough pill to swallow for the do-your-own-thing generation, and it comprises the primary scandal of true Christianity in the 20th century.[20]

How does Boff define the nature of the Scriptures? He states that they are not in themselves "the Word of God" but that the Bible is "a human word in which the divine Word is made concrete."[21] He believes that the Bible is full of myths (which he considers the best form for communicating religious truth) and that the New Testament in particular is more a creative invention of the early Church than a faithful account of the life of Jesus and the beginnings of the first Christian community.[22] Boff believes that the books of the Old and New Testaments are merely the result of devout men who "in the same way we do, approximated, speculated, theologized and allowed themselves to be oriented by their life of faith."[23] He compares the authors' activity in writing the books of the Bible with our ministry of preaching and teaching today. He states that, "without any great pretensions," we must see ourselves as part of the same process in which they were involved: observing life and speculating as to where God is at work in the natural events of history and what we should do to join Him there.[24] Of course, Boff is not actually saying that God does anything in history, since he is totally against the idea of the supernatural intervention of God in the affairs of men, but he chooses to write in these "mythical" terms (as if God were acting) because myth is the best vehicle for speaking of "the ineffable and the transcendent."[25]

Boff goes on to suggest that one of the worst problems in modern Christianity is the "erroneous" belief that it is possible to find specific models for conduct in Scripture. He insists that "Christ did not come to bring a cultural model ... He did not establish a rigid dogmatic, nor an ethic without heart," but to "create an atmosphere" of love and reciprocity.[26] He attacks the idea that the Christian faith can offer a "fixed model" and holds that "the Christian faith does not prescribe any fixed concrete application but rather, a specific *way* which should be present in any concrete application or posture."[27] He believes that Christianity has to do with "attitudes," not specific strategies, models, doctrines or ethics.[28] There is some truth to Boff's argument.

Evangelical Christianity has sometimes been guilty of being more specific than God's Word in its rules and regulations. The Scriptures do not decree the ideal structure for church government, the "one true way" to worship, which political party to vote for, the best economic organization of society, or many other specific areas of human involvement. But this is no reason to go as far as Boff has gone in denying all "fixed models" in Scripture.

A class of Colombian seminary students, when asked to look for biblical principles on the social ministry of the Church, came up with more than 70 passages in the New Testament dealing with poverty, wealth, justice, fair wages, hospitality, proper use of finances, social responsibilities of Christians, partiality in the church, duties of the rich to the poor, work ethics, help to the needy, obligations to widows and aid to those who are hungry, thirsty, naked, strangers, sick or imprisoned.

That does not exactly sound like a document that has no interest in leaving specific, fixed models for conduct for Christians. On the contrary, the New Testament is very clear in its teachings regarding the social responsibility of Christians. The main problem seems to be that there are too many Christians who are not willing to submit their daily lives to the plain teaching of God's Word. What would happen in Colombia, for example, if the New Testament's plain teaching regarding the duty of the rich to help the poor were actually put into practice by wealthy Colombians? A social revolution would result—without violence.[29] Likewise, if the "voluntary" poor, those who are poor not because of external factors over which they have no control but because of their own unwillingness to work, would practice Paul's injunction regarding work and industriousness, many would find themselves escaping the misery of poverty without joining Marxist revolutionary forces.[30]

Chilean economist Joseph Ramos, who made impres-

sive contributions to a study sponsored by the United
Nations Economic Commission on Latin America, has
made a convincing case that the major social problems
of Latin America could be solved without revolutionary
violence if government leaders would only follow more
sane and humane social policies.[31] Far from agreeing
with liberation theologians that God is at work in the
Marxist revolutionary movement to bring His kingdom
to Latin America, most Latin American evangelicals
believe that the only answer for their continent is a
spiritual revival. They long for a social/spiritual revolution similar to the Wesleyan revival in England in
which a priority on evangelism and conversion was
successfully wedded with a burning social conscience.
The revival substantially changed both the religious
and social life of England in one generation, avoiding
the destruction of violent revolution.[32] Most Latin American evangelicals see the problems the liberationists
have identified, but to solve those problems they seek
the means that are in agreement with the teachings of
God's Word.[33] Unlike Boff and Alves, they believe in the
"fixed models" presented by the New Testament to solve
the problems of injustice, oppression and poverty.[34]

Liberationists such as Croatto, Gutierrez and Miguez
Bonino share the same basic convictions already seen
in Alves and Boff. Croatto affirms, for example, that the
Bible is full of myths which were not meant by the
biblical authors to convey factual information but
rather to communicate "meaning" even though they
never really took place.[35] Croatto categorizes the following as mythical and not factual: all futuristic prophe-
cies, the supernatural inspiration of the Scriptures, the
fall of Adam and Eve, the flood, the plagues of Egypt,
the "passing over" of the Israelites by the death angel in
Egypt, the crossing of the Red Sea, the miraculous con-
quest of Canaan and many other Old Testament
events.[36] He also denies the factual character of many of
the miraculous events in the life of Christ.[37] Croatto
believes that the Bible has nothing normative to say to
guide us in living the Christian life today and that we

must "produce meaning" for ourselves and respond to
the challenges that face us.[38] Gutierrez affirms that we
must begin doing theology from a prior commitment to
revolutionary praxis, not the Scriptures, since a theology based on "truths established once and for all time"
always becomes "static and finally, sterile."[39]

Miguez Bonino makes the same kind of statement
when he affirms that Jesus did not leave us a "series of
ethical norms or moral principles" to direct us in our
decisions.[40] He criticizes the evangelical attempt to find
lasting guidelines for Christian conduct in Scripture,
since using the Bible "to derive from it correct Christian
action in all realms of the life of the Christian community" is an exercise in futility.[41] For Miguez the Scriptures
were never intended to give us specific guidelines for
conduct, they were intended only to offer us certain
"paradigms" or "parables" of God's action in history
which can help orient us.[42] The use of the word "para-
digm" instead of "principle" or "norm" is significant
since it reflects Miguez' conviction that the Scriptures
orient Christian action only in the most general, "indirect" way.[43] However, later in his writings Miguez suggests that "a really objective view of historical reality
requires significant hypotheses relating to 'constancies'
or (with all necessary caveats) 'laws' to direct our action
in history."[44] Here Miguez contradicts the very principle
with which he has so severely criticized traditional
theology—the concept that Christian action is based on
generalized principles taken from Scripture and applied
to modern life. But Miguez has radically changed that
process. Instead of finding these "constancies" or
"laws" in the interpretation of the Word of God, as traditional theology has sought to do, Miguez declares "for
some of us Marxism can be assumed at this level."[45]

It is amazing to see that when evangelicals take principles from God's Word for Christian action they are
often called Hellenistic, hypocritical, pharisaical and
naive, but when Miguez finds guiding principles for
Christian action in Marxist dogma, he is acclaimed as
progressive, relevant, practical and authentically

Christian.[46] In his theology the Bible gets sandwiched between Marxist analysis of social problems and Marxist strategies for solving those problems. God's Word becomes little more than a convenient source of illustrations and examples for Marxist dogma.[47] Scripture is swallowed up by ideology.

In conclusion we must say that for radical Liberation Theology the Bible is no longer the basis of theology, the rule for Christian faith and conduct. It is merely a collection of religious thoughts and remembrances in which important events, that enabled ancient communites to survive and liberate themselves from oppression and suffering, have been recorded with a great deal of mythical embellishment and legend-making. These documents, of little or no historical or normative value for the radical liberationists, still serve as an inspiration for modern liberationist Christians who seek to relate their faith to the issues of today. They also serve as illustrations and examples of Marxist precepts which have taken the place of biblical principles as the center of radical Liberation Theology. This view of the Bible's place in the Christian life is totally unacceptable to evangelical Christians both in Latin America and throughout the world.

Chapter 4, Notes

1. See, for example, John R. W. Stott, *The Lausanne Covenant* (Minneapolis: World Wide, 1975); Francis A. Schaeffer, *The Great Evangelical Disaster* (Westchester, Ill: Crossway Books, 1984), pp. 44-65; Kenneth S. Kantzer, "Unity and Diversity in Evangelical Faith," in David F. Wells (ed.), *The Evangelicals* (NY: Abingdon, 1975), pp. 39-52; and Bernard L. Ramm, *The Evangelical Heritage* (Waco: Word Books, 1973), pp. 140-150.

2. Carl F. H. Henry, "Insights on Liberation Theology," *United Evangelical Action*, Vol. 45, No. 2 (1986), pp. 4-6.

3. Carl F. H. Henry (ed.), *Revelation and the Bible* (Grand Rapids: Baker Book House, 1958), pp. 7-10; Kenneth S. Kantzer, "Unity and Diversity in Evangelical Faith," pp. 39-52.

4. See, for example, Donald Guthrie, *New Testament Theology*, pp. 947-948; *The International Critical Commentary* (1979), vol. 11, pp. 651-673; (*TICC*) *The Pastoral Epistles*, pp. 150-153; (*TICC*) *Epistles of St. Peter and St. Jude*, pp. 139-142; *The Expositor's Bible Commen-*

tary (1981), vol. 10, pp. 135-140; vol. 12, pp. 233-234; *Matthew Henry's Commentary*, vol. VI, pp. 466-469, 870, 1018-1019; *Calvin's Commentary* (1948 edition) on Romans, pp. 477-483; on the Pastoral Epistles, p. 324; on the Catholic Epistles, pp. 79-86; *Barnes' Notes* (1982), on Romans, pp. 290-297; on Titus, p. 281; on 1 Peter, pp. 145-148; John Wesley's *Explanatory Notes upon the New Testament* (1839 edition), pp. 398-399, 559, 612; *The Wycliffe Bible Commentary* (1962), pp. 1220-1221, 1395, 1447-1448; *The Wesleyan Bible Commentary* (1965), vol. V, p. 651; vol. VI, pp. 260-262. In Vol. V, pp. 80-82, there is an interesting exception to the examples cited above. In his discussion of Romans 13:1-7, Dr. Wilber T. Dayton, who was professor of New Testament Interpretation and Language at Asbury Theological Seminary when he wrote, allows for a "justifiable revolution . . . as a last resort" since "to forbid all forced reform or revolution might be to play into the hands of unscrupulous men and destroy the very law and order that should be defended" (p. 81). Dayton insists that "the emphasis of the Scripture is not to denounce the substitution of a legitimate for an illegitimate government," even though "many British and European commentators seem to interpret this passage as forbidding revolt against any *de facto* government (e.g., Godet, Moule, Denney)" (p. 81). I would agree with the interpretation of Godet, Moule and Denney, and note that Dayton's unfounded conclusion contradicts his own word-by-word analysis of what the text of Romans 13:1-7 actually says (pp. 80-81). Further, correct biblical interpretation is not based on the possible effects it may or may not have on "unscrupulous men."

5. Alves, "Theses for a Reconstruction of Theology," *Documents - IDOC* (October 31, 1970), p. 4.

6. Alves, "Theology and the Liberation of Man," in *In Search of a Theology of Development* (Geneva: Committee on Society, Development and Peace, 1970), p. 82.

7. Alves, "Theses for a Reconstruction of Theology," p. 14.

8. *Ibid.*

9. See, for example, 2 Timothy 3:16; 2 Peter 1:16-21; Matthew 5:17-18; Luke 16:16-17; Joshua 1:8; Joshua 22:5; 2 Samuel 23:1; Nehemiah 9:3, 30, 10:29; Deuteronomy 28:1, 29:1, 29; Psalm 119:1-8; Isaiah 55:6-11; Jeremiah 1:4-9; Hosea 1:1; Matthew 7:24-29; Mark 7:6-13; 1 Corinthians 2:6-13; Galatians 1:6-12; 1 Thessalonians 2:13; 1 Peter 1:10-12, 22-25; Jude 3; Revelation 1:1-2.

10. Alves, "El pueblo de Dios y la busqueda de una nueva ordenacion social," in Gustavo Gutierrez and others, *Religion, instrumento de liberacion?* (Barcelona: Marova y Fontanella, 1973), p. 133; and Alves, "Theses for a Reconstruction of Theology," p. 14.

11. Alves, "Injusticia y rebelion," *Cristianismo y Sociedad* II:6 (1964), p. 47.

12. Dennis F. Kinlaw, "Authority for the Church in Crisis," *Good News* (Oct.-Dec., 1970), pp. 23-27; Francis A. Schaeffer, *The Great Evangelical Disaster,* pp. 64-65.

13. Boff, *Liberating Grace* (Maryknoll: Orbis Books, 1979), pp. 35-36.

14. Boff, *Hablemos de la Otra Vida* (Santander: Editorial Sal Terrae, 1978), p. 17.
15. Boff, "Las imagenes de Jesus en el cristianismo liberal del Brasil," *Cristianismo y Sociedad* XIII:46 (1975), pp. 33-34.
16. *Ibid.*
17. *Ibid.*, p. 33.
18. Carl F. H. Henry, "The Modern Revolt Against Authority," in Henry, *God, Revelation and Authority* (Waco: Word Books, 1979), pp. 7-23; Francis A. Schaeffer, *How Should We Then Live?* (Old Tappan, NJ: Fleming H. Revell, 1976), pp. 167-181, 205-227.
19. *Ibid.*
20. *Ibid.*
21. Boff, *Teologia del Cautiverio y de la Liberacion* (Madrid: Ediciones Paulinas, 1978), p. 43.
22. Boff, "Las imagenes de Jesus en el cristianismo liberal del Brasil," p. 41.
23. Boff, *Hablemos de la Otra Vida,* p. 17.
24. Boff, *Eclesiogenesis: las comunidades de base reinventan la Iglesia* (Santander: Sal Terrae, 1980), pp. 78-79; and Boff, "Las imagenes de Jesus en el cristianismo liberal del Brasil," p. 33.
25. Boff, *Jesucristo el Liberador* (Bogota: Indo-American Press, 1977), p. 186.
26. *Ibid.*, p. 60.
27. Boff, "Salvacion en Jesucristo y proceso de liberacion," *Concilium* 96 (1974), pp. 386-387.
28. *Ibid.*
29. *Los evangelicos en Colombia: un analisis critico* (Bogota: CEDEC, 1978), p. 199; and Jaime Ortiz Hurtado and others, *Hermeneutica, Biblia y Liberacion* (Medellin: Seminario Biblico de Colombia, 1984), pp. 3, 73-75.
30. Michael Novak, "Why Latin America Is Poor," *The Atlantic Monthly,* March, 1982, pp. 69-71.
31. *Ibid.*, pp. 71-75.
32. See, for example, the Latin American perspective in Emilio Nunez, *Liberation Theology* (Chicago: Moody Press, 1985), pp. 277-290; and the Wesleyan model in Timothy L. Smith, *Revivalism and Social Reform* (NY: Harper & Row, 1957), pp. 148-177; and Bernard Semmel, *The Methodist Revolution* (NY: Basic Books, 1973), pp. 3-4, 110-113, 127-131, 138-142, 231-232 (note 134).
33. See, for example, Emilio Nunez, *Liberation Theology,* pp. 78-82; Samuel Escobar, "El Reino de Dios, la Escatologia y la Etica Social y Politica en America Latina," in C. Rene Padilla (ed.), *Fe Cristiana y Latinoamericana Hoy* (Buenos Aires: Certeza, 1974), pp. 127-156; and Pedro Arana Q., "Ordenes de la Creacion y Responsabilidad Cristiana," pp. 169-184, in the same work.
34. *Ibid.*
35. Croatto, *Historia de la Salvacion* (Buenos Aires: Ediciones Paulinas, 1970), pp. 23-24, 29-31, 200; Croatto, *Hermeneutica Biblica: para una teoria de la lectura como produccion de sentido* (Buenos Aires: La Aurora, 1984), p. 48; and Croatto, *Liberacion y Libertad:*

pautas hermeneuticas (Lima: Centro de Estudios y Publicaciones, 1980), pp. 28-30 and 45-47.
36. Croatto, *Historia de la Salvacion,* pp. 23, 73-74, 122, 172-175; and Croatto, *Hermeneutica Biblica,* pp. 45ff, 85.
37. Croatto, *Hermeneutica Biblica,* pp. 53-54.
38. *Ibid.,* pp. 27-42.
39. Gutierrez, *Teologia de la liberacion: perspectivas,* p. 37.
40. Miguez, "Fundamentos teologicos de la responsabilidad social de la Iglesia," in *Responsabilidad Social del Cristiano* (Montevideo: ISAL, 1964), p. 29.
41. Miguez, "The Struggle of the Poor and the Church," *Ecumenical Review* XXVII:1 (January, 1975), p. 24.
42. Miguez, "Un Dios que actua y renueva la iglesia," in *America Hoy* (Montevideo: ISAL, 1966), p. 39.
43. *Ibid.*
44. Miguez, *Doing Theology in a Revolutionary Situation,* p. 97.
45. *Ibid.*
46. See, for example, Jose Miguez Bonino, "The Struggle of the Poor and the Church," *Ecumenical Review* XXVII:1 (1975), pp. 24-40; Miguez' *Christians and Marxists,* p. 30; and his *Doing Theology in a Revolutionary Situation,* pp. 88-90; also, Jose P. Miranda, *Marx and the Bible,* pp. 248-265; Jose S. Croatto, "La religiosidad popular," *Cristianismo y Sociedad* 47 (1976), pp. 40-43; Rubem Alves, "Confessions: On Theology and Life," *Union Seminary Quarterly Review* XXIX:3/4 (1974), pp. 181-186, and his "From Paradise to the Desert" in Rosino Gibellini (ed.), *Frontiers of Theology in Latin America,* p. 301; Alves' "Giving Account of Faith," *Study Encounter* 77 XI:2 (1975), p. 2; and his "Theology and the Liberation of Man," in *In Search of a Theology of Development,* p. 77; and James Barr, *Fundamentalism* (London: SCM Press, 1977), pp. 1-89.
47. Miguez, "The Struggle of the Poor and the Church," pp. 38-39; Miguez, *Doing Theology in a Revolutionary Situation,* pp. 86-87, 97; and Miguez, *Christians and Marxists,* pp. 41, 114-115, 118-119, 121-125, 128-132.

Is Radical Liberation Theology Violent?

This is the second most crucial question in the evaluation of radical Liberation Theology. It is their espousal of revolutionary violence which separates the radical liberationists from the more moderate Latin American theologians who often use some liberationist rhetoric while stopping short of promoting armed revolt. Also, there is no clearer point at which the radical liberationists resist the authority of the Scriptures than at this point of espousing revolutionary violence. To deal with this central issue we will attempt to answer six crucial questions about violence and radical Liberation Theology.

1. *Do radical liberationists condone the use of violence, and if so, why?*

Radical liberationists *do* condone the use of violence as what they call "counter-violence." Alves puts the argument clearly when he affirms that:

Violence is power that oppresses, makes man unfree. Counter-violence is power that breaks the old which enslaves, in order to make free. Violence is power aimed at paralysis. Counter-violence is power aimed at making man free for experimentation. . . .[1] Violence is power used to dominate. When the slave decides to become free, he is rejecting the validity of violence. His project is liberation, not domination. But he knows that the master will not give up his power willingly. The masters do not liberate the slaves. The slaves liberate themselves, and in this act they liberate the masters for a new type of relationship. If they have to reject violence, as the basic master-slave relationship, they have to exercise counter-violence, that is, power used against violence, power directed toward liberation.[2]

In this way Alves has been able to argue that the initial violence is the institutionalized violence of corrupt governments which violently oppress and repress the populace of their nations. Thus, argues Alves, the reaction of liberationists and other revolutionaries to this first violence is "counter-violence," which is power used to redress wrongs committed by violent, repressive governments. For Alves the government's institutionalized violence is reprehensible, while the insurrectionists' counter-violence is justified and necessary.

Hugo Assmann argues that the "fundamental intention of [Christian] love [is] doing away with violence;"[3] but that sometimes it is necessary to use "violence to overcome violence."[4] He goes on to state that that documents of the CELAM II meetings in Medellin make it clear that the Roman Catholic hierarchy of Latin America has accepted the concept of "institutionalized violence" as a faithful description of what is going on in Latin America today. Therefore the only moral response to this observation is support of counter-violence to eliminate the first violence committed against the poor and the weak.[5]

Jose Miguez Bonino picks up this same argument, insisting that "we are always . . . actively in the field of action of the violence—repressive, subversive, systematic, insurrectional, evident, hidden . . . *My* violence is direct or indirect, institutional or insurrectional, conscious or unconscious. But it is violence."[6] He argues that no one can find a "neutral position" from which to look at this problem: if you do nothing you are in fact supporting the institutionalized violence of the oppressors in power.[7] This argument voiced by Miguez (and many other liberationists) is so powerful that we need to stop and consider it for a moment. In effect they are saying that if you are not for us you are against us; if you do not support the revolution, then by your inertia you are automatically supporting the status quo. They charge Christians who do not commit themselves to the revolution with being committed *de facto* to the oppressive social order in power, since the lack of their opposition keeps the present government in power. If this is true, everyone can be divided into two groups: revolutionaries and counter-revolutionaries, committed and opposed, activists and reactionaries.

Evangelical Christians cannot accept this line of argument. A former student of mine who has become a liberationist chaplain to the guerillas in the mountains of Colombia once asked me, "If you had lived in Nicaragua prior to the Sandinista revolution, who would you have supported, Somoza or the Sandinistas?" I answered, "I would have supported the kingdom of God, which is neither Sandinista nor Somocista, but judges both of them." Although this answer sounds like a huge evasion to the liberationists, as biblical Christians we have no other answer. Our final loyalty can never be to our own country, our own political party, our own ideology or even our own family—our final loyalty belongs only to Jesus Christ and His kingdom. He judges men like Somoza for their greed, their corruption and their violence, but He also judges the Sandinistas for their power-seeking, their cruelty and their violence. No nation, no political group, no army, no system escapes the judgment of the kingdom of God. If as Christians we are to participate in God's prophetic denunciation of sin wherever it may be found, we cannot give our final loyalty to any group, but we must stand "over against" everything in society, denounce it when it violates God's eternal principles and praise it when it follows them.

The other main argument used by liberationists to

condone the use of violence is that of "revolutionary
necessity." Assmann observes that, "if we analyze history, we will be able to prove that there has not been up
to now any authentically revolutionary movement that
has been able to dispense with recourse to violence in the
physical sense of killing of men."[8] Miguez calls revolutionary violence the "midwife" of liberation,[9] and declares his agreement with Marx and Lenin that violence
is "necessary because there is no other way of overturn-
ing [the capitalist] system."[10] In short, their argument is
that Christians must condone the use of violence because it is necessary for the success of the revolution,
and the success of the revolution is necessary for the
liberation of the oppressed. In other words, the end justifies the means. Although many of the liberationists
express personal apprehensions about unleashing revolutionary violence in their continent because of the destruction, hate, injustice and plunder it can bring with
it, in the final analysis they must approve of it because it
is the only way to bring about the revolution they seek.[11]
For the radical liberationists, these two arguments of
"violence vs. counter-violence" and "revolutionary
necessity" are sufficient to convince them that revolutionary violence must be condoned, albeit hesitantly.

2. *Do they believe there is a biblical basis for the use of violence?*

As we have said before, pure liberationist theory does
not permit them to base their actions on biblical teaching; nevertheless, they seem to wander back into old
patterns of submission to the biblical text whenever it
suits their purposes. Croatto, for example, attempts to
show that the Exodus illustrates the need for violence to
destroy resistant injustice and oppression. He explains
that, in the situation of domination, "justice is a radical
good, that demands of *love* (although it may appear
paradoxical) a *violent* action."[12] He does not need to deal
with the problem the Exodus example presents—the
fact that God is the author of the violence, not the

Hebrews—since he believes that any report of God's intervention in the event is purely mythological.[13]

Miguez argues for violence by explaining that there are two general perspectives on violence in the Bible— the priestly and the prophetic. The priestly perspective stresses the status quo, order and harmony; the prophetic stresses liberation and the destruction of all limits.[14] He believes that the prophetic mode must take priority over the priestly view. Thus violence for liberation must be given priority over violence for preservation of the status quo.[15] Miguez also argues that the Bible does not present violence as an either/or principle which forbids all violence or justifies all violence. Instead it views violence as "concrete acts which must be carried out or avoided in view of a result, of a relation, of a project indicated by the announcement-commandment [of God]."[16] Miguez summarizes the Bible's view on "acts of acceptable violence" by describing them as "means to break out of conditions (slavery, vengeance, arbitrariness, oppression, lack of protection, usurpation) that leave a man, a group of people, or a people unable to be and act as responsible agents ... in relation to others, to things, to God."[17] Here we see Miguez' desire to use the Bible without allowing the authority of the Bible to exercise its control over his actions. By "summarizing" the biblical evidence in such a way that it supports his view, he has in effect appealed to the Scriptures without actually submitting his theology to them. He has also muddied the waters a bit by indiscriminantly using both the Old and New Testaments as if there were no differences between them, when of course there is a great difference, especially regarding the use of violence. Both Croatto and Miguez' use of Scripture in this argument illustrates clearly their lack of belief in its historical truthfulness and their rejection of the Bible as norm in their theology.

3. *If Christ was not a violent revolutionary, why should Christians be violent revolutionaries?*

This question causes serious problems for some of the

radical liberationists. They seem determined to answer it one way or the other. It is obvious that anyone who claims to be a follower of Jesus Christ, a "Christian," whose theology urges one to live in a way patently contradictory to the way Jesus Christ lived, has serious problems in his/her theology. Croatto faces this dilemma by arguing that those who try to identify Jesus with the revolutionary Zealot movement of His day "do a disservice to the cause of liberation."[18] Croatto clarifies that Jesus refused to join the Zealots, not because He opposed their revolution against Rome, but because He opposed their nationalistic goals of setting up a Jewish state founded on oppressive, legalistic religious laws.[19] Rather, affirms Croatto, Jesus' program for brotherly love, condemnation of religious domination, rejection of emperor worship, preference for the poor and confrontation with all oppressive authorities began a revolutionary process that could have effects for all people, regardless of national origin.[20]

Croatto goes on to suggest that "the *reality* that we live is different from that of the Jews of the Palestine of Jesus," and thus "our possibilities of 'reading' it are different and produce another kind of awareness-building."[21] He holds that the appearance of the "social sciences" (especially Marxism) has given us new ways to see reality that neither Jesus nor His contemporaries had, and because of that, we are enabled to see a revolutionary "reserve-of-meaning" in the text not seen in this way before now.[22] In this sense for Croatto, although Jesus was not a revolutionary, the process He began can be "re-read" in a revolutionary way today thanks to the perspectives offered to modern Christians by the "social sciences."

When Juan Luis Segundo considers this problem, his answer is to affirm that the Christian message in Jesus' day "was not directed to men for all time, but was inserted in history in that particular moment."[23] He makes it clear that it is wrong to try to set up the "Christ event" as the final criterion for Christian conduct, since there are many cultural and historical differences between the present time and the first century.[24] With this simple wave of the hand Segundo dismisses the problem of the contradiction between Jesus' life, teaching and example and the call to revolutionary violence in radical Liberation Theology. Although evangelicals would agree that there are vast cultural and historical differences between the first and twentieth centuries, they would also insist that the life of Jesus constitutes a model and example that transcends those differences.

The liberationist who has taken this problem most seriously is Jose Miguez Bonino. He has admitted that "Jesus did not identify himself with the struggle of the Zealots of his time for the liberation of his country,"[25] but he argues that although Jesus did not "enroll himself with the Zealots, . . . he did not seem to have left any doubt about whether he was on the side of the poor and oppressed or the power structures . . . of his time."[26] For Miguez, Jesus "was judged and executed as a subversive" because he "was rightly . . . accused of having taken the side of the oppressed against the constituted religious and political authorities."[27] In this way Miguez portrays Jesus as a non-violent "subversive" who was on the side of the oppressed against the oppressors, encouraged His followers to violent revolt and was *rightly* judged and executed for that crime. That is not what the biblical record says about Jesus. Correcting this error, Martin Hengel, in his excellent study of this question, concludes:

> Was Jesus a revolutionist? That was our question. We can answer it only with a *sic et non,* with yes *and* no. He cannot be party to those who—then as now—seek to improve the world by violence, a violence which begins with a hate-filled defamation and escalates to bloody terror, to torture and mass murder, where each party shifts all the blame on the opponent . . . . Jesus pointed a quite different way with *agape:* the way of nonviolent protest and willingness to suffer, a way which deserves more fully the designation 'revolutionary' than does the old primitive way of violence. During his activity of one or two years he was a greater force in world and intellectual history than all

the agents of revolutionary violence from Spartacus and Judas the Galilean till today.... In this sense, one can quite correctly call Jesus a revolutionary, and this can be underscored with superlatives. But perhaps precisely today, *when the word 'revolution' has become so cheap and hip, even among theologians,* we should refrain from calling him a revolutionary.... The truth does not lie in our 'interpreting' the figure of Jesus to accord with the latest fashion of our time—a process in which 'interpreting' all too easily becomes a falsifying; but truth lies in this, that our life is molded and fashioned by him.[28]

Jesus was no revolutionary or "subversive" in the modern sense. In fact He often purposely rejected this way and made it clear that He would have nothing to do with it.[29] Miguez' portrayal is an example of what Albert Schweitzer has described as modern theologians' ability to find their own thoughts in Jesus, in that "each individual created Him in accordance with his own character."[30] But this is not the end of Miguez' argument.

Miguez seems to sense that his "Jesus-the-subversive" argument will not win the day, so he shores it up with one of the most amazing examples of theological sleight-of-hand ever attempted. In effect Miguez admits that Jesus did not join in the revolutionary movements of His day, but he uses the very non-involvement of Jesus as motivation for the involvement of Christians in revolutionary movements today! Miguez argues that Jesus did not participate in the revolutionary movements of His day because He was "renouncing the exercise of divine power to settle men's affairs."[31] Thus Jesus' refusal to participate in revolution did not signal a "spiritualization of religion" in which His followers should not participate in revolution either, but it signaled a "secularization of politics" in which Jesus made it clear that He was leaving the way open for men to work out their own political problems without His help.[32]

For Miguez, Jesus' non-violence and non-revolutionary life proves that man must conduct his own affairs and create his own history without expecting any divine intervention.[33] In this classic example of theological sleight-of-hand, Miguez has shown that Jesus' rejection of involvement in revolution is proof of His desire that His followers be revolutionists!

The way in which Miguez is forced to treat Scripture on this question indicates the embarrassing problem it is for radical Liberation Theology. This theology, while purporting to be a *Christian* theology, urges the followers of Jesus Christ to adopt methods and practices which are openly contrary to the example of His life and the norm of His teaching. Certainly this is one of the most serious hurdles radical Liberation Theology must attempt to leap.

4. *Can violence be an expression of Christian love?*

Jose Severino Croatto has said that "love and violence are opposite, but connected poles" since "love can be violent when the loved object cannot be retained or recuperated without the use of force."[34] He insists that when domination and exploitation of one group over another exists, "justice is a radical good, that demands *of love* (although it may appear paradoxical) a *violent* action."[35] Love and violence go together when not using violence would be an unloving denial of the rights of life and liberty to the oppressed.[36]

Jose Miguez Bonino has written extensively on this subject. The following summary of his views on love and violence is taken from his book, *Room to Be People* (the numbers in parentheses correspond to the page numbers in that book):

> Love [is] . . . a concrete and effective commitment to the real need of another or others who have been placed in our sphere of action (p. 45). [In Matthew 25] acts of love (which every Jew had learned to recognize since infancy): to give food to the hungry, to give drink to the thirsty, to clothe the naked, to visit and care for the imprisoned, the stranger, the sick . . . . There is no act of love that is lost, without an eternal future . . . . His kingdom is the triumph of single-minded and

active love. Every act which corresponds to this kingdom has eternal permanence, is made of the same material as the kingdom itself, and therefore is included in it. In the New Testament there is little speculation about death and the hereafter. What is constantly repeated is that the love of Jesus Christ is permanent and that death cannot end it (pp. 52-53). The life of Jesus is a life of love and *therefore* of conflict. Or better yet, his love is involved in the conflicting conditions of human life in which it cannot help but take part. This love is involved in the often radical tensions we find in our current international situations, with rich countries and poor countries, oppressors and oppressed, and in the conflicts present within our own societies (p. 61). True love cannot remain as intention, in the abstract; it demands to be made concrete. However, in order to do this one must choose *a way* to concretize it . . . . When love is confronted with human need in its widest sense, it must choose a strategy, a political and economic orientation, and become involved in the forms of organization. If love stops short of manifesting itself in this way, it can only with great difficulty be called love (p. 63).

Miguez insists that the ethic of Christian love must make its presence felt in the struggle for liberation "by insisting on counting carefully the cost of violence, by fighting against all idolization of destruction and the destructive spirit of hate and revenge, by attempting to humanize the struggle, by keeping in mind that beyond victory there must be reconciliation and construction. But [Christians] cannot block through Christian scruples the road clearly indicated by a lucid assessment of the situation . . . [nor should they be guilty of] weakening through sentimental pseudo-Christian slogans . . . the will among the oppressed to fight for their liberation."[37] For Miguez and many of the other radical liberationists, participation in revolutionary violence is the natural response of Christian love to the misery and suffering of the oppressed. For evangelicals it is necessary, because of our submission to the authority of the Scriptures, to go beyond an "end-justifies-the-means" mentality. Such thinking argues that if there is a problem and there is a solution possible that pretends to provide a better life for most of the people in a country, then as Christians we must use whatever means will bring about that solution. Evangelicals' belief in the authority of God's Word determines that both "ends" and "means" must be judged according to that standard. It is one thing to say that the Bible sets the goal of peace and well-being for all people, but it is quite another to say that the Bible affirms the use of revolutionary violence to reach that goal. Evangelicals cannot make the easy identification between love and violence that the radical liberationists have been able to make.

5. *Can the "just war" concept be expanded to the concept of a "just revolution"?*

Liberationists are very fond of using the argument that since most Christians approve of the "just war" concept, then oppressed people have a right to extend that to a "just revolution" concept.[38] If conditions exist under which war can be justified as right and acceptable to Christians, then why can't criteria be set up to indicate when a revolution is right, acceptable and justifiable? This is a very strong argument and merits careful consideration. It sounds like this: If the people of a nation find that those who govern them have become cruel, unjust, arbitrary, oppressive, exploitative, tyrannical and murderous, then they have a right to revolt against that government and replace it with one that is more just. The Vatican accepts this logic, calling revolution "the last recourse to put an end to an evident and prolonged tyranny that gravely imperils the fundamental rights of the person and dangerously damages the common good of the country."[39] Although the Vatican, represented by its "Sacred Congregation for the Doctrine of the Faith," emphasizes that non-violent action is superior to armed revolt, it does open the door for Christian participation in armed revolt as a last recourse in a desperate situation. Can evangelicals accept this position on a "just revolution" as well?

Again, for evangelicals this question must be decided
by scripture. First, we need to answer the question, "Can
the just war concept be defended biblically?" Of course
the answer to that question lies far beyond the scope of
this book. Christians have been debating that issue for
centuries without coming to unity on what the Bible
does or does not teach on the subject. For our purposes, it
is probably sufficient to say that most Christians have
at least tacitly accepted the just war concept in some
way. Most Christians do not oppose war in and of itself.
They may bemoan the destruction and loss of life, but in
general modern Christians accept war as a "necessary
evil."[40] Clearly Christians who oppose all use of violence
can easily reject the "just revolution" as well as the "just
war" concept, but many Christians who accept the "just
war" idea reject the idea of a just revolution on very solid
biblical grounds.

There are at least three passages in the New Testament that deal directly with this question: Romans 13:1-
7, Titus 3:1-8 and 1 Peter 2:13-17. These passages show a
remarkable unity in proclaiming Christians' duty to
submit to the authority of the government of their
nation or locality. Romans 13:1 reads, "Let every person
be in subjection to the governing authorities. For there
is no authority except from God, and those which exist
are established by God." Titus 3:1 reads, "Remind them
to be subject to rulers, to authorities, to be obedient, to be
ready for every good deed." 1 Peter 2:13-14 commands,
"Submit yourselves for the Lord's sake to every human
institution, whether to a king as the one in authority, or
to governors as sent by him for the punishment of evil-
doers and the praise of those who do right." As
evangelicals we believe that these passages represent
an inspired commandment given by God through Peter
and Paul, the two chief apostles of the early Christian
Church. They concur in their mandate that Christians
should be subject to the authority of those who govern
them.

Several questions have arisen from the study of these
passages. For example, is the submission asked for here

an *absolute* submission or is it conditional? Do Christians have to submit to *anything* the government authorities demand or are there limits to Christian submission? Is it wrong for Christians to protest unjust treatment at the hands of corrupt authority figures? Can Christians support revolt against unjust tyrants who illegally threaten their lives?

Fortunately the books of Acts gives ample evidence of just how far that submission should go. Both Peter and Paul found themselves in many conflicts with civil and religious authorities who were opposed to the gospel. The classic case occurs in Acts 4 where Peter and John are brought before the Jewish Council of Jerusalem and the religious authorities (they also had civil authority in these cases) who "commanded them not to speak or teach at all in the name of Jesus" (Acts 4:18). Peter and John answer, "Whether it is right in the sight of God to give heed to you rather than to God, you be the judge; for we cannot stop speaking what we have seen and heard" (Acts 4:19-20). After being released, Peter and John continue to speak out, disobeying the Council's order. They are arrested again, freed by an angel of the Lord and arrested a third time for preaching and testifying in public. When the high priest reminds them, "We gave you strict orders not to continue teaching in this name, and behold, you have filled Jerusalem with your teaching, and intend to bring this man's blood upon us," Peter and the apostles answer, "We must obey God rather than men" (Acts 5:28-29). This is certainly not a picture of *absolute* submission to the authorities. Later, Paul used his rights as a Roman citizen to avoid being killed by his Jewish enemies who wanted him placed under their authority by the governor Festus (Acts 25). Paul's "appeal to Caesar" is evidence of the way he used Roman law to protect himself from civil and religious authorities who treated him unjustly.

Several important observations must be made regarding the submission of Peter and Paul to the authorities. First, their submission was not absolute. When they felt the authorities were acting unjustly against them, they did not give absolute submission but protested this unjust treatment and asked for justice according to the law.

Second, they openly and publicly refused to submit to the authorities when they commanded them to cease testifying, that is, to cease doing something that God Himself had commanded them to do. Peter's "we must obey God rather than men" shows their response to authorities who asked them to do something that would be disobedient to God's expressed will.

Third, they never used violence against the authorities, even when they were very unjustly treated (even when they were in danger of being killed). They did not physically resist those in authority even when they knew that those in power were acting completely unjustly.

Fourth, Peter and Paul never suggested any form of revolt and demonstrated their respect for rulers and authorities, even in the face of unjust treatment. Although they did not submit absolutely to them, they never encouraged anyone to revolt violently.

In the light of these biblical principles, can evangelicals accept the idea of a "just revolution?" The answer is no. In light of the teaching of the New Testament and the example of the Apostolic Church, Christians are commanded to submit to those in authority in a way that is not absolute but does exclude the possibility of Christian participation in armed revolt. We will not do whatever the authorities command us to do if God prohibits it; we will not cease doing whatever they prohibit if God commands it; but we will not rise up against them in violent revolt, though they treat us unjustly or even kill some of us. No absolute submission, but no armed revolt—that is the biblical Christian's position.

6. *Should Christians oppose all revolutions?*

No other question tests the resolve of American evangelical Christians more than this one. It is one thing to say that we oppose revolutions in which Marxists are attempting to take over countries in Africa, Latin America or Asia. But would we also oppose a revolution against the leaders of the Soviet Union if the revolutionaries wanted to impose a democratic system in the USSR? Would we oppose a group of Cuban "freedom fighters" who wanted to invade Cuba, oust Castro and restore democratic freedoms to that island nation? Of more immediate importance, do we support the revolution being carried on by the Contras against the Marxist Sandinista regime in Nicaragua?

Surely no question more clearly shows our absolute submission to the authority of God's Word than this one. If we accept the norm of Romans 13, Titus 3 and 1 Peter 2 as the last word on Christian support of revolution, we must be willing to say *no* to all revolutions without regard to how many of our compatriots support them, how advantageous they are to the citizens of those nations involved or how much benefit they might bring to the United States.

We must remember that Paul was not saying that Christians should submit only to just government authorities. He was writing to Christians living in Rome, the seat of the powerful and often unjust Roman Empire. Paul's assertion that God is behind even unjust authorities echoes the words of Jesus as He stood before Pilate in what must be the most unjust and corrupt judgment ever given (since Jesus was perfectly innocent). When Pilate threatened Jesus saying, "You do not speak to me? Do You not know that I have authority to release You, and I have authority to crucify You?" Jesus answered this cruel, unjust, hypocritcal Roman governor saying, "You would have no authority over Me, unless it had been given you from above" (John 19:10-11). Was there ever a more *justifiable* motivation for armed revolt than the travesty of a trial perpetrated against Jesus? He said to Pilate, "My kingdom is not of this world. If My kingdom were of this world, then My servants would be fighting, that I might not be delivered up to the Jews; but as it is, My kingdom is not of this realm" (John 18:36).

If Jesus did not allow the disciples to use violence to free Him from the injustice of the rigged trial that cost Him His life, will there ever be an injustice great enough to warrant Christian participation in and support of armed revolution? I think not. If we are to answer the challenge of radical Liberation Theology, we must be completely consistent in our obedience to God's Word, even when it goes against the patriotic demands of our own nation. Only Christians who have authentically given their ultimate loyalty to Jesus Christ, His kingdom and His Word have a right to question the "justified" counter-violence the liberationists are demanding.

Chapter 5, Notes

1. Alves, *A Theology of Human Hope,* p. 125.
2. Alves, "Violence and Counterviolence," in Samuel Shapiro (ed.), *Cultural Factors in Inter-American Relations* (South Bend: Notre Dame Press, 1967), p. 38.
3. Hugo Assmann, *Teologia desde la praxis de la liberacion* (Salamanca: Ediciones Sigueme, 1973), p. 204.
4. *Ibid.*
5. *Ibid.,* p. 205.
6. Miguez, Violence and Liberation," *Christianity and Crisis* 32 (July, 1972), p. 169.
7. *Ibid.*
8. Assmann, *Teologia desde la praxis de la liberacion,* p. 203.
9. Miguez, *Doing Theology in a Revolutionary Situation,* p. 115.
10. *Ibid.,* p. 125. (It should be noted that Marx considered certain exceptions to this necessary use of violence.)
11. Assmann, *Teologia desde la praxis de la liberacion,* p. 205; Juan Luis Segundo, *De la sociedad a la teologia* (Buenos Aires: Ediciones Carlos Lohle, 1970), pp. 144 and 151-154; Miguez Bonino, *Doing Theology in a Revolutionary Situation,* pp. 125-128, and "The Struggle of the Poor and the Church," in *Ecumenical Review* XXVII:1 (January, 1975), p. 43. It should be noted here that Leonardo Boff does not seem to advocate violent revolution in his published works to date, only "political science of a rebellious cast."
12. Croatto, *Liberacion y libertad,* p. 52.
13. *Ibid.,* p. 45.
14. Miguez, "Violence and liberation," in *Christianity and Crisis* 32 (1972), p. 169.
15. *Ibid.,* p. 171.
16. *Ibid.,* p. 170.
17. Miguez, *Doing Theology in a Revolutionary Situation,* p. 118.

18. Croatto, *Liberacion y libertad,* p. 99.
19. *Ibid.,* pp. 99-100.
20. *Ibid.,* pp. 100-103.
21. *Ibid.,* p. 103. (The term "awareness-building" is a rough translation of the Spanish "concientizacion," which is literally "concientization" and signifies the process of awakening in the oppressed the consciousness of what their situation is and what are the hidden dynamics behind it that cause their suffering [i.e., capitalist exploitation and oppression]. The idea of "building this awareness" comes fairly close in English to this concept and is used in many translations of liberationist literature.)
22. Jose Severino Croatto has borrowed the concept of "reserve of meaning" from the French hermeneutical philosopher Paul Ricoeur, who believed that there are hidden meanings behind a biblical text which it has accumulated through the centuries of interpretation and re-interpretation of the original event on which the text was based (see Ricoeur's *Conflict of Interpretation* and *History and Truth*). Croatto took this idea from Ricoeur and sharpened it by saying that at the core of every significant biblical event is a liberation of some people from oppression and slavery, and that therefore, it is possible to find a hidden liberationist meaning behind all important biblical texts (see Croatto, *Liberacion y libertad,* pp. 16-19).
23. Segundo, *De la sociedad a la teologia,* p. 153.
24. *Ibid.,* pp. 153-154.
25. Miguez, *Doing Theology in a Revolutionary Situation,* p. 122.
26. *Ibid.,* pp. 123-124.
27. *Ibid.*
28. Martin Hengel, *Was Jesus a Revolutionist?* (Philadelphia: Fortress Press, 1971), pp. 32-35 (in spite of some of Hengel's liberal tendencies, this is a very helpful study).
29. Note Jesus' rejection of the "Messiah-Revolutionary" role in: John 6:1-15; Matthew 26:50-57; John 18:33-36; and Acts 1:1-8; and His rejection of the use of violence in Luke 6:27-36.
30. Albert Schweitzer, *The Quest of the Historical Jesus* (New York: Macmillan, 1961), p. 4.
31. Miguez, *Doing Theology in a Revolutionary Situation,* pp. 123-124.
32. *Ibid.*
33. *Ibid.,* p. 125.
34. Croatto, *Liberacion y libertad,* p. 50.
35. *Ibid.,* p. 52.
36. *Ibid.,* pp. 51-52.
37. Miguez, *Doing Theology in a Revolutionary Situation,* p. 128.
38. For example, see Assmann, *Teologia desde la praxis de la liberacion,* pp. 203-206.
39. Sacred Congregation for the Doctrine of the Faith, "Instruccion sobre Libertad Cristiana y Liberacion," paragraph 79.
40. See J. G. Davies' *Christians, Politics and Violent Revolution* (London: SCM Press, 1976), pp. 147-187, for his argument in favor of the "just war" and "just revolution" concepts. As can easily be seen, I

disagree almost totally with his perspective, but I believe he communicates the argument in one of the clearest presentations that has been written.

CHAPTER 6

Is Radical Liberation Theology Marxist?

In the course of this chapter we must answer at least three basic questions. First, is radical Liberation Theology a Marxist plot to infiltrate the Christian Church using theologians who are actually "wolves in sheep's clothing"? Second, is radical Liberation Theology specifically committed to Marxism, or is it only committed to the poor and whatever can help them? Third, if they accept Marxism as part of their theology, do the radical liberationists accept it critically or uncritically?

Many people have accused radical Liberation Theology of being nothing more than a Marxist plot to infiltrate and control the Christian churches of the Third World. Liberationists have been accused of being "Leninist theologians," and some Roman Catholic leaders have even charged that the document written by Dom Helder Camara for CELAM II proved that "the communists have infiltrated the ecclesiastical hierarchy."[1] At the same time, Cuban president Fidel Castro has stated that "there is no contradiction between religion and revolution . . . Marxists and Christians can be strategic allies."[2]

Is radical Liberation Theology part of a Marxist infiltration plot? I think not. The theologians promoting radical Liberation Theology do not seem to be Marxists covertly trying to worm their way into Christian churches to pervert them, but rather they are sincere individuals who have come to believe that Marxist revolution is the only hope for the struggling masses of Latin America. Surely they would not be so open in their statements regarding Marxism if they were taking part in an infiltration plot. They are definitely not atheists, which of course disqualifies them from full adherence to Marxist dogma.[3] All of them have come up through the ranks of their respective churches to places of leadership and major responsibility. So the possibility that any of them could be Marxist "plants," placed in the church to undermine it and lead it into Marxist commitment, is very remote indeed.

The second question is much more controversial: Is radical Liberation Theology committed to Marxism or only committed to the poor and whatever will help them? Many observers of radical Liberation Theology would characterize it as a sincere, concrete Christian commitment to the poor and their liberation. These observers see radical Liberation Theology as a truly Christian movement which sounds different from Western Christianity only because of the problems it has to deal with in Latin America. Liberation Theology has often been presented, especially in the United States, as a Christian option for the poor which speaks a slightly different language than North American Christian faith because it comes out of a desperate, violent situation.[4] As a United States evangelical seminary professor shared, "We'd all be liberationists if we had to live where they live." Although there are theologians in Latin America to whom this more moderate description could be applied, they are a class apart from the radical liberationists described in this book.

Dom Helder Camara, archbishop of Recife, Brazil, uses liberationist terms to describe the plight of the poor in Latin America, but he does not advocate armed revolution as the solution to the social problems of the continent. Camara has described the "spiral of violence" in

Latin America in which the "established violence" of injustice to the poor attracts the violence of revolt. This in turn attracts the violence of repression which leads to more intense revolt, and the spiral of violence continues to escalate.[5] Camara has suggested what he calls "liberating moral pressure," similar to Martin Luther King's methods, to break the spiral of violence and avoid the destruction of armed revolution.[6] He has been rejected by the radical liberationists for his peaceful solution, but he has a tremendous following, especially among the youth of Brazil.

Mortimer Arias is another moderate who, as Methodist bishop of Bolivia, has been identified with the liberationist analysis of the oppression and misery of Latin America. But he proposed peoples' movements and an integral ministry of evangelism and social concern as the Christian answer.[7] These men are not representative of the radical Liberation Theology movement. What sets them apart is that, although they are deeply concerned about the plight of the poor and have recognized the evils of exploitation and oppression in Latin America, they have recommended peaceful solutions rather than violent, revolutionary ones. Latin American evangelicals find it easy to identify with men like Camara and Arias.

On the other hand, radical Liberation Theology is not just a new way of talking about concern for the poor—it is a theological revolution that seeks to change everything about the Christian faith from the way we read the Bible to the way we think about God. Alves explained in a 1973 article that Marxism is the very center of this theological revolution. It provides the radical liberationist with the proper analysis of social problems, the key to understanding the Scriptures and the best strategy for solving those problems.[8] Miguez has described the same role for Marxism in radical Liberation Theology in a positive, affirming way. He states that for him Marxism is "the unavoidable historical mediation of Christian obedience."[9] Gustavo Gutierrez believes that Marx has offered the best analysis of capitalism and exploitation and the most effective way to defeat them—revolution.[10] He commends the new strategic alliance between Christians and Marxists to fight against their common enemy—the oppressors.[11] Croatto chides Western Christians for praying for the conversion of the Soviets and suggests that instead they could have spent their time more profitably "asking themselves why Russia is communist, cooperating in the advent of an authentic, profound socialism, seeing in Marxism a 'sign of the times' which evokes the 'subversive memory' of the Exodus in Christians."[12]

Boff and Miranda are not as open as Alves, Gutierrez, Miguez and Croatto in their support of Marxism. Boff asserts that Christian theology does not need to join any ideology in order to liberate the poor,[13] but, in statements regarding how to "do theology," he insists that theology must always be a "second step" after analysis of the present situation of society.[14] In answer to the question about what kind of social analysis Christian theology should start with, Boff answers, "a cultural reading grounded primarily on sociology, economics, and political science of a rebellious cast."[15] But what is this "rebellious" reading of social realities he suggests? It is a reading of reality grounded on a brand of sociology, economics and political science which promotes revolution. It accepts the "theory of dependence" which claims that the conditions of poverty and suffering in Latin America are a direct result of the way the United States and other rich nations exploit the poor countries of the world. The theory insists that the only way to break that dependence is through liberation and the establishment of a socialist society.[16] It is vehemently opposed to international capitalism which it considers the cause of poverty, high infant mortality, marginalization, disease, unemployment, oppression and lack of schools and hospitals in Latin America.[17] It accepts socialism as the only solution to the social problems of Latin America.[18] Although Boff refuses to accept the "Marxist" label on his theology, it is apparent that the "rebellious reading" of reality he describes is essentially

Marxist.

Mexican radical liberationist Jose Porfirio Miranda actually criticizes Liberation Theology for its allegiance to Marxism. He complains about the way Liberation Theology has substituted social analysis for the Scripture as the center of theology and argues that, in doing so, it has ceased to be theology and become an ideology.[19] However, in spite of all of his protests to the contrary, Miranda is the most Marxist-influenced of all of the radical liberation theologians. His 1971 work, *Marx and the Bible,* is devoted to 12 carefully developed proofs of the essential oneness of Marxism and Christian doctrine. In his 1978 book, *El Cristianismo de Marx* (The Christianity of Marx), he does his best to try to prove that "at the height of his maturity Karl Marx was a Christian and believed in God," and his "message is Christian in a real, substantial sense."[20] Although Miranda dedicates a great deal of his writings to detailed studies of Scripture, it is all too obvious that his goal of proving the oneness of Christianity and Marxism colors all of his studies.

Having shown the commitment to Marxism in the radical Liberation Theology of Alves, Gutierrez, Miguez, Croatto, Boff and Miranda, we must answer the final question of this chapter. Do they accept Marxism uncritically or critically? That is, do they follow Marxist dogma slavishly or do they evaluate it, accepting only the parts they judge to be correct? The answer of course is that they are all critical of Marxism to varying degrees. Miranda is the least critical of the group, not only accepting Marxist dogma but also trying to harmonize biblical doctrine with it. Gutierrez and Croatto have some, but very little, critique of Marxism in their theologies. The most critical radical liberationists are Boff, Alves and Miguez. They see major problems in Marxist dogma that Christian faith can and must correct. Still, their acceptance of the basic premises of Marxism gives their theology a definite Marxist tilt.

Miguez has probably offered more critical reflection on the relationship between liberationist Christianity and Marxism than any other liberation theologian. He has suggested four main areas of relationship: (a) Christians and Marxists share the view that knowledge is not theoretical contemplation but active involvement; (b) they also share a commitment to human solidarity; (c) Christians can accept the Marxist program for liberation with some minor corrections; and (d) Christians and Marxists differ in their view of the source and power behind solidary love—for Christians it is Jesus Christ while for Marxists it is the masses alone.[21]

Miguez believes that Christians can join the Marxist revolutionary movement, accepting and overcoming the Marxist criticism of religion, helping to reduce the use of violence, refusing to accept the totally materialist view of life and giving counsel in the ethical decisions that will need to be made during the "dictatorship of the proletariat."[22] The detailed way in which Miguez presents his understanding of the proper relationship between Christians and Marxists gives ample evidence of the radical liberationists' concern for carefully defining the Christian-Marxist "strategic alliance" which they are proposing.

Chapter 6, Notes
_____

1.   Enrique Dussel, *Historia de la Iglesia en America Latina* (Barcelona: Nova Terra, 1974), p. 228.
2.   *Time*, Vol. 115, No. 5 (February 4, 1980), p. 48.
3.   See, for example, Andre Dumas' cogent article in 1965, presenting the concept that atheism is central and essential for Marxism in *Cristianismo y Sociedad* 8 (1965), pp. 53-62, as contrasted in the same issue with Joseph Hromadka's view that the "anti-religious ideals in socialism are accidental" and "secondary" and therefore, not essential for Marxism (pp. 62-69).
4.   See, for example, the "watered-down" version of Liberation Theology presented in the following works: Justo L. and Catherine Gunsalus Gonzalez, *Liberating Preaching* (Nashville: Abingdon, 1980); Theo Witvliet, *A Place in the Sun: An Introduction to Liberation Theology in the Third World* (Maryknoll: Orbis Books, 1984), especially pp. 118-150; James Thomas O'Connor, *Liberation: Towards a Theology for the Church in the World* (Rome: Catholic Book Agency, 1972); and Esther and Mortimer Arias, *The Cry of My People* (NY: Friendship Press, 1980).
5.   Helder Camara, *Spiral of Violence* (London: Sheed and Ward,

1979), pp. 25-39.
6. *Ibid.*, p. 55.
7. Mortimer Arias, *Salvacion es liberacion* (Buenos Aires: La Aurora, 1973), pp. 11-15, 19-29, 90-121.
8. Alves, "Marxism as the Guarantee of Faith." It should be noted that the Marxism Alves and other radical liberationists refer to is the "neo-Marxism" of Althusser and other modern Marxists.
9. Miguez, *Doing Theology in a Revolutionary Situation*, p. 98.
10. Gutierrez, *Hacia una teologia de la liberacion* (Bogota: Indo-American Press, 1971), pp. 24-25.
11. *Ibid.*, p. 54.
12. Croatto, *Liberacion y libertad*, p. 75.
13. Boff, *Teologia del Cautiverio y de la Liberacion*, p. 85.
14. Boff, *Liberating Grace*, pp. 65-66.
15. *Ibid.*
16. *Ibid.*, pp. 66-67. Again, Boff does not *openly* advocate violent revolution, but his discussion of taking sides in the "conflict" tends toward that application.
17. Boff, *La Vida Religiosa en el Proceso de Liberacion* (Salamanca: Sigueme, 1980), pp. 9-10.
18. Boff, "Funcion de los Religiosos en la Liberacion Integral del Hombre," in Instituto Teologico de Vida Religiosa, *Responsabilidades eclesiales y sociales de los Religiosos* (Madrid: Publicaciones Claretianas, 1978), pp. 189-191.
19. Miranda, *El Ser y el Mesias* (Salamanca: Sigueme, 1973), pp. 78-79.
20. Miranda, *Marx Against the Marxists* - translation of *El Cristianismo de Marx* (London: SCM Press, 1977), back cover.
21. Miguez, *Christians and Marxists*, pp. 118-119.
22. Miguez, *Christians and Marxists*, pp. 128-132; and Miguez, *Doing Theology in a Revolutionary Situation*, p. 97.

CHAPTER 7

What Do The Liberationists Believe?

In 1971, under the leadership of the "Group of 80" (a gathering of Chilean liberationist priests inspired by Allende's socialist victory in their homeland), priests from Argentina, Brazil, Bolivia, Colombia, Peru and Chile met together to plan for a Latin American convocation of all Christians committed to socialism as the only way to construct a just society on their continent. In April of 1972 more than 400 Protestant and Roman Catholic liberationists from 26 nations met in Santiago, Chile, to plan how to support the revolutionary movements in their respective countries in response to the Group of 80's invitation. This was the largest meeting of liberationists ever brought together and has still not been equalled. Each person invited had to fulfill the requirement of being actively involved in a "real life option for revolution" as a Christian in Latin America. The main work of the Encounter (entitled "Christians for Socialism") was to make detailed plans for Christian participation in revolutionary movements in each nation of Latin America and to formulate a united declaration of liberationist faith. The declaration elaborated in this Encounter is without a doubt the clearest, most extensive expression of liberationist faith ever written. The following "Liberationist Catechism" is based directly on the Spanish text of the document published by the Christians for Socialism Encounter in 1972. The numbers in parentheses correspond to the numbered paragraphs in the original Spanish text. The best answer to the question, "What do the liberationists believe?" is to allow them to speak for themselves in this summary of their own document.

A LIBERATIONIST CATECHISM

"We wish to identify ourselves clearly as Christians who, on the basis of the process of liberation in which our Latin American peoples live and of our practical and real commitment to the construction of a socialist society, think through our faith and revise our attitude of love for the oppressed" (1).

I. *What is the problem behind the Latin American situation of suffering?*

A. Dependency and Domination:
1. The continued wealth of the rich nations of the North is derived from the exploitation of the poor nations of Latin America (2).
2. The nations of Latin America are maintained in dependent capitalism by rich and powerful national elites who benefit economically from the unjust, oppressive situation (4).
3. These national elites maintain their own power and the submission of the masses through violent repression (5).
4. The dominant elites have produced a culture which presents man chiefly in individualistic terms so that private property can be defended and love can be reduced to the interpersonal level to prevent a proper understanding of the structural injustices of society

(59).

5. The dominant classes teach the masses to resign themselves to their fate, be reconciled with their class enemies, accept the government's violence as necessary and reject revolutionary violence as anti-Christian (60, 61).

6. The dominant classes are allied with the Church in seeking the pacification and submission of the masses and use the Christian faith to justify their exploitation of the masses (56, 63, 66).

B. Capitalism:

1. Because the nations of Latin America have adopted capitalism, their modes of production have produced an unjust classist organization of society (16).

2. Capitalism perpetuates its hold on Latin America through the national bourgeoisie who are in alliance with the institutional Church (18).

3. When that policy fails, the forces of capitalist imperialism consolidate their power by supporting repressive fascist dictatorships which maintain control through torture, persecution and terror (19).

4. The capitalist imperialists seek to prevent the union of Christians and Marxists in order to paralyze the revolutionary process in Latin America (21).

5. The capitalists use mass communications and popular education to convince the masses of the necessity of the present unjust order as a protection from the horrors of communism (23, 60, 61).

C. Class Struggle:

1. Class struggle is the foundation of all correct scientific analysis of society (48).

2. Class struggle is caused by the private ownership of the means of production (49).

3. Class struggle takes place within the Church as well (40).

4. Some Christians have been naive in their political involvement because they have ignored the structural mechanisms of class struggle and have tried to base

their political activism on humanistic concepts such as human dignity and liberty (53).

5. The ethical blocks that Christians have against the conflictive nature of class struggle can be eliminated only through involvement with the proletariat in liberating praxis (44).

6. The alliance between Christianity and the dominant classes must be broken in order to renew the conflictive and revolutionary character of authentic Christianity (63).

II. *What is the solution to the Latin American situation of suffering?*

A. Revolution:

1. The only solution to the problem of injustice, oppression and domination is that the oppressed nations of Latin America unite to overthrow the power of imperialistic capitalism (3).

2. Socialism cannot be brought about through appeals and denunciations. The exploiting classes must be overthrown (11).

3. There is no neutral position in the face of revolution (29).

4. The proletariat masses are the vanguard of the revolution (38).

5. There is an urgent need to unite all the revolutionary forces of the continent (36).

6. False models of economic development are being used to distract the masses from the need for revolution (22).

7. As Christians, we do not wish to offer a Christian alternative to the present revolutionary movement, but rather we wish to unite with it (8).

8. The commitment of Christians to the revolution is having a great impact on the entire continent (41).

9. Priests and pastors who have discovered that political action is necessary if the love for the oppressed demanded by the gospel is to be made effective are making a positive contribution to the Latin American revo-

lutionary process (45).

10. Christians can make a positive contribution to the revolution once the interaction between faith and revolutionary praxis has brought out previously unknown elements in Christianity (65).

11. Revolutionary praxis contributes to the Christian faith through critique of its historical complicity with the dominant classes (66).

12. The Christian faith's authentic life is liberating praxis, but it can experience that praxis only through involvement with organizations directly active in the revolution (67).

13. In their revolutionary commitment, Christians learn that the transforming love of God can be lived out effectively only in confrontation and antagonism (68, 69).

14. Christian theological thought then becomes a new reading of the Bible and Christian tradition which restates the basic concepts of Christianity in such a way that they encourage and support the revolution (70, 71).

B. Marxism:

1. Chiefly through Marxist analysis the masses are being awakened to the need to take power (32).

2. The Cuban Revolution and Chilean socialism signal a return to the origins of Marxism and a critique of traditional Marxist dogmatism (31).

3. There is a growing realization of the need for a strategic alliance between Christians and Marxists to carry out a common historical project of liberation (46).

C. Socialism:

1. It is necessary to transform in a radical way all the structures of society to create a socialist order in which there will be neither oppressors nor oppressed (7).

2. Socialism can be achieved only through revolution (11).

3. There is no third way between capitalism and socialism (25).

4. Revolutionary forces must make socialism their goal

(26).
5. Socialism is not a collection of historical dogmatisms, but a critical theory which is constantly being informed and revised by historical events (52).
6. We have committed ourselves to socialism because after a rigorous and scientific analysis of the situation we have concluded that it is the only effective way to combat imperialism and free us from the slavery of dependence (10).

Conclusions:
1. The liberation which Christ effects is carried out in historical liberating events but cannot be reduced to them since political liberation is only part of Christ's total liberation (9).
2. The commitment of this encounter can best be summarized in the words of Che Guevara: "When Christians dare to give an integral revolutionary testimony, the Latin American revolution will be invincible" (72).

CHAPTER 8

Are They Right Or Wrong?

The study of radical Liberation Theology should be an enriching experience for any evangelical Christian. The liberationists' criticism of traditional theology makes many points that are obviously right, and evangelicals need to listen to those points and be willing to change accordingly. Liberationists criticize traditionial theology for all too often communicating Christian doctrine in terms of Greek philosophy and religious thought. For example, evangelical Christian faith has sometimes been taught as the pilgrimage of the soul trying to escape its captivity in the "evil" body. This idea is not from Scripture, which speaks of the redemption of the body and its resurrection, but from Greek dualism which taught that the soul was good and the body, evil like all matter. Christian faith is not an attempt to rid the soul of the evil body but a life of bringing both body and soul under the lordship of Christ and the control of the Holy Spirit.[1] Radical Liberation Theology has pointed out this dualistic, Greek tendency in traditional theology and has served us well in doing so.

The liberation theologians have also pointed out the exaggerated individualism of some forms of evangelical faith. For some evangelicals the only important thing in life is their own personal salvation. They spend most of their time enjoying their own personal experience with the Lord and seeking to improve it. They seem to have little concern about the spiritual welfare of others, much less for their physical welfare. They are on their way to heaven and, as a popular evangelical chorus in Latin America says, "If someone else doesn't go, what's that to me?" This kind of exaggerated individualism is not a part of biblical Christianity and must be eliminated.

The Liberation Theology movement has been quick to point out the lack of social ministry in traditional Christian churches. Evangelicals have been particularly guilty at this point. As we said before, the New Testament has a great deal of teaching about the social responsibility of the church to the poor, the sick, the widowed, the imprisoned, the naked, the thirsty, the hungry and all those in need. The proponents of the "social gospel" in past decades have reduced Christianity to nothing more than meeting others' needs, while many evangelicals, in their reaction against the "social gospel," have often gone to the other extreme—almost completely eliminating social ministry from the life of the church. As evangelicals we do not believe that physical aid is the end-all of the gospel and a substitute for evangelism, but at the same time, if we are to be biblical Christians, we must recognize and fulfill our responsibility to those around us who are in need, "to all men, and especially to those who are of the household of the faith" (Galatians 6:10). The liberationists, in their extreme position on social action, have helped many Latin American evangelicals see their own extreme position of being divorced from the Christian social responsibilities outlined in Scripture. In that sense they have helped us return to a more biblically-balanced, integrated ministry of evangelism and social ministry.[2]

Liberation Theology has also stressed the need for "orthopraxis"—right action. Although traditional theology has stressed "orthodoxy" (right belief), the New Testament makes it clear that right belief without right action is dead (see James 2:17). We are called to be "doers of the word, and not merely hearers" (James 1:22). Of course, the liberationists have gone too far in the other direction—they are "doers" without the foundation of right belief. But that must not distract us from our need to hear this timely reminder that it is easier to *believe* the right things than it is to *do* the right things. It is easier to believe in the power of prayer than it is to discipline ourselves daily to pray. It is easier to believe in the authority of the Bible than it is to study it and submit our lives to it on a day-by-day basis. It is easier to believe that "somebody ought to help him" than it is to roll up our sleeves and actually help! Biblical "orthopraxis" must be the natural outcome of biblical "orthodoxy" or there will be spiritual deadness.

Finally, the liberationists have pointed out traditional theologians' obsessive fear of Marxism ("Marxophobia") and their often uncritical support of capitalism. As a missionary I suppose that this is where Liberation Theology hit me the most. I had never seen how critical I was of Marxism and how uncritical I was of capitalism until I began to read Liberation Theology. I should add that I am still more critical of Marxism than I am of capitalism, but Liberation Theology helped take the blinders off my eyes so I could see that, as a Christian, I am not committed ultimately to Marxism or to capitalism. I am committed to the kingdom of God. We must criticize both systems where they are wrong and praise both systems where they are right. This is not easy because of the way many of us have been conditioned by our political and ideological upbringing. However it is something that we must learn to do if we are to be faithful to our highest commitment, which is to Jesus Christ and His kingdom, so that those who see us will observe that our final loyalty is not to our own country, political system or ideology, but that our loyalty goes beyond all these things to the one "kingdom which cannot be shaken" (Hebrews 12:28). Liberationists, Marxist students, guerrilla soldiers and citizens of socialist countries around the world must know that, as American evangelical Christians, our goals for world evangelization cannot be identified with the foreign policy of the State Department of the United States. As the liberationists have gone too far in their allegiance to Marxist dogma, so have many evangelicals in their criticism of the liberationists. These evangelicals have revealed their basic criteria for judgment as "what's best for America" and the perpetuation of the democratic free enterprise system, rather than the demands of the kingdom of God which judges both Soviet socialism and U.S. capitalism.[3]

It is obvious that, as we carry out this critique of Marxism and capitalism, we are not speaking of some kind of "moral equivalency" theory in which some leftist-thinking Americans want to affirm that the United States has been just as sinful, reprehensible and destructive as the forces of international communism. This is patently untrue and reflects the "flip side" of the more typical uncritical acceptance of capitalism by Americans. Although the kingdom of God judges both Marxism and capitalism equally, the results of that judgment are certainly not equal—the suffering, injustice, violence and deaths caused by Marxists far outweigh those caused by capitalists and thus must be judged more severely by the standards of the kingdom of God. Nevertheless, capitalists are far from exempt from the judgment of God for the sins that have been perpetrated against humanity in the name of economic progress or national security.

The radical liberationists have been right in at least parts of their assertions, and we should listen to them and do all we can before the Lord to bring our living of the Christian faith in line with the teachings of God's Word. At the same time they have also been wrong in some very important areas, and we can learn from their mistakes as well. Their most fundamental error is their denial of the authority of God's Word for Christian faith and practice. Obedience to the Word of God as taught by Jesus and transmitted to the Church through His apostles is the cornerstone of all New Testament Christian faith. Jesus taught that the wise man would hear His words and do them. He criticized the pharisees and scribes for "teaching as doctrines the precepts of men." Jesus said, "If you abide in My word, then you are truly disciples of Mine" (John 8:31). In one of His last talks with His disciples He told them, "If anyone loves Me, he will keep My word; and my Father will love him, and We will come to him, and make our abode with him" (John 14:23). Jesus' last commandment to the apostles was to go throughout the whole world making disciples, "teaching them to observe all that I commanded you" (Matt. 28:20). The apostles were called "eyewitnesses and servants of the Word." The first Christian church in Jerusalem was characterized by its devotion to the "apostles' teaching." Luke describes the growth of the new churches founded by the first Christian missionaries, saying, "the word of the Lord was growing mightily and prevailing" (Acts 19:20). Paul describes his ministry of evangelism and church planting by saying, "When you received from us the word of God's message, you accepted it not as the word of men, but for what it really is, the word of God, which also performs its work in you who believe." The New Testament closes with the apostle John, who "bore witness to the word of God and to the testimony of Jesus Christ."[4] To deny this heritage and accept the idea that the Bible, the foundation of our faith, is the word of men and not the Word of God is to deny the most basic and fundamental doctrine of Christianity. This basic error spawns all of the other errors in radical Liberation Theology.

Once the liberationists had banished the Word of God as the final norm for doctrine and practice, they committed a second major error in substituting Marxist dogma in its place. Having lost the focal point and authoritative base of God's Word, they made Marxism their authority and committed themselves to its view of history, its analysis of the dynamics of social reality and its revolutionary solution to the problems of oppression, class struggle and exploitation. Once Christian faith had been passed through the filter of Marxist dogma, the resulting "praxis-doctrine" had little in common with the inspired teaching of the Scriptures. Radical Liberation Theology is "reductionist;" it reduces the Christian faith to a program for revolutionary violence and filters out a great deal of the teaching of Jesus and of the apostles because it does not fit in with the program for revolutionary violence liberationists have in mind.

One other major error of radical Liberation Theology is the doctrine of "universalism," the belief that all mankind will eventually be saved.[5] Rubem Alves sought the "incognito Church" in the world, declaring that God will save all of His creation "not just some individuals."[6] Gustavo Gutierrez holds that in Christ "all has been saved;" salvation covers all who have been created.[7] He believes that all men share the same destiny, a "convocation to salvation," and insists that Christ is at work in all men whether they know it or not, forming an "anonymous Christianity."[8] As a result, Gutierrez feels that Christians should abandon a "quantitative view of salvation" and adopt a "qualitative view," which declares that "the man who opens himself to God and others, even without having a clear consciousness of it, is saved."[9] Jose Severino Croatto believes that "the non-Christian discovers God in a silent way—the unknown God—and manifests Him in his way of living."[10]

These theologians believe that all history is one and that God is at work redemptively in all people, whether they believe in Him or not.[11] The universalism of the radical liberationists has allowed them to focus all their attention on bettering peoples' lives. If all will eventually be saved regardless of what they believe about Jesus Christ, then evangelism is a waste of time and the best thing Christians can do is make sure that everyone has the best life possible on the road to ultimate salvation in Christ. However, according to the Word of God, that is not the case. There is a heaven, there is a hell and there will be a judgment. Jesus taught that. Those who turn their back on this central teaching of the Scriptures do so at their own (and others') peril. Universalism is a heresy and cannot be tolerated in biblical Christianity.

It is this false doctrine which has made radical Liberation Theology so one-sided in its understanding of humanity's problems and how to solve them. The liberationists' single-minded over-emphasis on bettering physical conditions stems from their belief that humanity's eternal destiny is secure, regardless of what a person believes. This is not the teaching of Jesus Christ or the teaching of the prophetic/apostolic testimony of the Scriptures.

One other lesson that evangelicals can learn from radical Liberation Theology has to do with the needs demonstrated by the wide acceptance of this theology, even among some evangelicals. The popularity of Liberation Theology seems to show that Christians today are looking for a fuller, more integrated faith. They seem to want a faith which can speak to the major issues of our day—both spiritual and social—in a practical way. The evangelicals in this group are generally not looking for a "social gospel" approach, but they are looking for an evangelistic, biblical expression of faith accompanied by a compassionate, loving, biblically-based social outreach to those in need. The Church must respond positively to this earnestly felt need which is in complete harmony with the full message of Scripture.

Also, the wide acceptance of Liberation Theology reveals many people's desire to hear the Christian faith speak out on some of the most controversial subjects of our day—poverty, injustice, oppression, misery, dehumanization, violence, terrorism, Marxism, capitalism, classism, economics, international politics, wealth, power and many others. Evangelical theology should always be open to the questions people are asking. There are biblical answers to those questions. The problem is that often certain questions have not been asked of the biblical text before, so it takes some disciplined work to find true biblical answers. This is the positive side of the relationship between biblical interpretation and social analysis—allowing social analysis to ask the questions but answering those questions on the basis of the authoritative norm of Scripture.

One of the most exciting elements in the popularity of Liberation Theology is the possibility of using "liberation" as a concept for organizing biblical evidence. The "liberation" described in the Scriptures is much deeper, more complete and more exhaustive than the political liberation described in radical Liberation Theology. The Exodus *is* central to much of Old Testament theology, and its model of slavery, deliverance and freedom is used in the Old and New Testaments as one of the main descriptions of the salvation that God offers man. Today we have a wonderful opportunity to speak to the heart-cry of millions of people by proclaiming the truth of God's plan for humanity in terms of a *biblical* theology of liberation, which would respond to the modern individual's search for liberation and also be faithful to God's message in Scripture.

Finally, the challenge of radical Liberation Theology has forced many evangelicals to re-think some of the models in Christian history in which evangelistic fervor and social ministry were effectively wedded. At this point I believe my own Wesleyan heritage can offer a significant contribution. The Wesleyan revival and the early Methodist Church which resulted from it offer an excellent example of a burning evangelistic zeal accompanied by a compassionate, active social concern.[12] Study of this model and others like it will enrich modern evangelical attempts to live out the gospel of Christ more faithfully and effectively.

The liberationists are right in some areas and wrong in others. We can learn a great deal from their criticisms of us and from our own evaluation of their errors, but perhaps the greatest lessons are taken from the elements of modern society in which the liberationist message has found its greatest emotional response—the poor, the downtrodden, the compassionate, the would-be world-changers. If evangelicals can learn to speak the gospel in such a way that, without perverting it, they answer these people's questions and show God's way of solving their problems and directing their passion, the latter part of this century could witness an evangelical awakening that would rival any seen up to now in the history of the Church.

Chapter 8, Notes

1. See, for example, Boff, *Hablemos de la Otra Vida,* pp. 32-33; Gutierrez, *Teologia de la liberacion: perspectivas,* p. 102; and Miguez, "Theology and Liberation," *International Review of Mission* LXI:241 (1972), p. 69.

2. For an excellent study of the relationship between evangelization and social ministry, see the paper, "Evangelism and Social Responsibility," published by the Lausanne Committee for World Evangelization and the World Evangelical Fellowship, 1982.

3. See, for example, "The Marxist-Revolutionary Invasion of the Latin American Churches," published by the Church League of America, 1972; Walter W. Benjamin, "Liberation Theology: European Hopelessness Exposes the Latin Hoax," *Christianity Today* XXVI:4 (February 19, 1982), pp. 21-23; and William E. Matheny, "Keeping the Main Thing the Main Thing," *Fundamentalist Journal* II:9 (October, 1983), pp. 50-52 (especially note his approving citation of David Breese's definition of Liberation Theology on p. 51). Currently a great deal of debate is going on in the United States among "free market theologians" who are attempting to prove that: (a) capitalism is the only viable Christian option; (b) socialism is unacceptable because it is economically unfeasible, ethically immoral and politically destructive of personal liberty; and (c) Christians should promote a "free market system" around the world to solve all nations' economic ills (see Ronald Nash, editor, *Liberation Theology,* his chapter entitled "The Christian Choice between Capitalism and Socialism," pp. 49-67). These "free market theologians" would counter Liberation Theology with what Nash refers to as a call for a "new liberation theology" that will "recognize the irrelevance and falseness of socialist attacks on capitalism, that will unmask the threats that socialism poses to liberty and economic recovery, and that will act to move existing economic institutions and practices closer to the principles of a free market system that alone offers the hope of economic progress" (Nash, ed., *Liberation Theology,* p. 49). In answering Nash's call, I must suggest that: (a) what he is asking for is not a "theology" but an economic/ideological manifesto; (b) not all of the "socialist attacks on capitalism" are irrelevant and false; and (c) the view that a "theology" should be formed "to move existing economic institutions and practices closer to the principles of a free market system" reveals the flip side of the same kind of ideological commitment seen in radical Liberation Theology in which the gospel is reduced to a political, economic, ideological program. The fact that Nash champions a system which has a better track record than Marxism in terms of morality, protection of individual liberties and religious toleration, makes his absolute commitment to capitalism more understandable but no more acceptable. Christian theology cannot be reduced to an ideological

option! It is greater than that and must always stand "over against" *every* man-made system, regardless of how beneficent or tyrannical they may appear to be. Nash finds it all too easy to accept the greed and materialism of the capitalist system as "natural human desires" (pp. 62-66) without bringing them under the judgment of the gospel for what they are—sins. Nash suggests that capitalists' "greed for someone else's property must be channeled into the discovery of products or services for which people are willing to exchange their holdings" (pp. 61-62), while Jesus charges Christians to "Beware, and be on your guard against every form of greed" (Luke 12:15).

The "free market" or "democratic capitalism" debate among Christians is being carried on by some who seem to be as radical as Nash (such as Franky Schaeffer, ed., *Is Capitalism Christian?*) as well as by others who are much more cautious in their evaluations. Michael Novak's works reflect this less-strident analysis of the weaknesses of socialism and the relative strengths of capitalism (for example, *The Spirit of Democratic Capitalism*). Those interested in studying Nash's arguments in greater detail should see his *Poverty and Wealth* and *Social Justice and the Christian Church*.

Clark Pinnock, in "A Pilgrimage in Political Theology" (Nash, ed., *Liberation Theology,* pp. 101-120), seems to express my concern when he states: "Should we go so far as to say that the Bible supports this economic policy [democratic capitalism]? I think we should be cautious in this area. If the Bible does teach this policy, it is strange why we did not discover it earlier. It is also risky to tie the Scriptures to any such system, thus repeating the radical mistake of regularly linking it to socialism" (p. 115). Although he then proceeds to enumerate some biblical insights which "are at least compatible with [free] market practices," he is careful to temper this with critical analysis: "instead of presenting a spiritual alternative to the Soviet barrenness, we have ourselves fallen into self-centered materialism which reduces everything to a monetary value" (p. 116). That is the kind of critique we must produce as evangelical Christians—critique which does not reduce the gospel to an economic/ideological option but, at the same time, does use biblical principles to judge all systems, denouncing wrong aspects and recognizing good ones. Although Pinnock ends up opting for capitalism over socialism as the more ideal political/economic system (as I do), he does not confuse that economic preference with Christian theology as the liberation theologians on one side, and Nash on the other, have tended to do. That precarious balance is surely the call to all evangelical Christians who wish to uphold the absolute independence and authority of God's Word and, at the same time, make its message relevant in analyzing the conflicting ideologies of our day.

4. Matthew 7:24-27; Mark 7:6-8; John 8:31; John 14:23; Matthew 28:19-20; Luke 1:2; Acts 2:42; Acts 19:20 (and 6:7, 12:24); 1 Thessalonians 2:13; Revelation 1:2.

5. For a helpful discussion of the problem of universalism in Liberation Theology, see Orlando Costas' *The Church and Its Mission: A Shattering Critique from the Third World* (Wheaton: Tyndale, 1974), pp. 257-260.

6. Alves, "Injusticia y rebelion," pp. 47-48.

7. Gutierrez, "Apuntes para una teologia para la liberacion," in *Cristianismo y Sociedad* 24/25 (1970), p. 16.

8. Gutierrez, *Teologia de la liberacion: perspectivas*, pp. 105-108.

9. *Ibid.*, p. 196.

10. Croatto, *Liberacion y libertad*, p. 21.

11. For example, see Boff's *Teologia del Cautiverio y de la Liberacion*, pp. 83-84; and Gutierrez' *Teologia de la liberacion: perspectivas*, p. 199.

12. See Timothy L. Smith, *Revivalism and Social Reform* (New York: Harper and Row, 1957); Howard A. Snyder, *The Radical Wesley* (Downers Grove: Inter-Varsity Press, 1980); and Bernard Semmel, *The Methodist Revolution* (New York: Basic Books, 1973).

CHAPTER 9

World Council Of Churches And Liberation Theology

In the past few years several articles have been written on the World Council of Churches (WCC) alleging misconduct and "communist collaboration" on the part of WCC officials. Some of these reports have been factual while others have been rather sensationalistic. It is often difficult to determine exactly what the staff of the WCC thinks about a given issue, since so much of the WCC literature reflects the opinions of the denominational representatives to the Council and not the position of the WCC staff itself.

In the summer of 1981 I spent 10 days at the WCC headquarters in Geneva, Switzerland, doing research for my dissertation at Cambridge University on Liberation Theology. I was given full access to the library and archive facilities of the WCC and was able to do detailed research concerning the WCC position on Liberation Theology. I studied the documents written by WCC staff members in preparation for the assembly and commission meetings of the Council. The description that follows relates what I discovered regarding the WCC staff's increasing commitment to radical Liberation Theology.

In 1968 the Fourth Assembly of the WCC met in Uppsala, Sweden, to consider the theme, "all things new." The WCC staff urged delegates to see that conversion is not primarily the salvation of the soul but is a commitment to become involved in what God is doing in history. One of the WCC Bible study authors suggested that the quality of new life in Christ is manifested in national struggles for justice in our world today since God Himself stands behind the efforts of humanity to change society.

As evangelicals we affirm that from the biblical perspective conversion *is* personal salvation. Granted that conversion is seen afterwards in service to humanity, but it is the cause of that service, not its effect. Further, God does not stand behind all the efforts of man to change society. He opposes many of them.

In 1972 the Commission on World Mission and Evangelism of the WCC published a collection of essays to prepare delegates for their "Salvation Today" meetings in Bangkok. The introduction to the collection makes its direction clear. Delegates are informed that to discover the meaning of salvation today, it is not enough just to restate the Bible's teaching on the subject since God's salvation is not a static reality that can be seen in the Scriptures. Instead it is a dynamic, ongoing historical event in which God is working out His purposes for humanity and the world.

The author also affirms that the proper context in which both to understand and proclaim the mission of the Church and salvation is now the modern quest for political, economic, cultural and personal liberation. He also declares that fellowship within the Church and non-Christian fellowship between individuals are both created by Christ and equally form a part of God's plan of salvation for the world. In this way WCC leaders had begun an attempt to shift delegates from the biblical view of salvation, in terms of forgiveness of sins and new life in Christ, to a new perspective that sees salvation as a superior quality of life in which the well-being of all is achieved through political and economic struggles for liberation from oppression. This is, of course, the key tenet in radical Liberation Theology.

The collection of essays which follows has some traditional Christian emphases, but it also contains 12 essays which definitely reflect the convictions of radical Liberation Theology. Some of the authors are Latin American liberation theologians and spokesmen such as Ernesto Cardenal, Nestor Paz and Camilo Torres. The views of Marxists like Julius Nyerere, Roger Garaudy and Ignazio Silone are presented even though some of them are atheists. A communist Chinese scientist is portrayed in an essay entitled "Saved by Mao," which testifies how the writings of Mao helped him to see the error of his ways and change.

These 12 texts combined would present the central problems of Latin America (and the world) as exploitation and oppression and the solution to those problems as Marxist revolution. All of this is presented within a discussion of what salvation means today. Clearly the staff of the WCC, although not yet totally given to radical Liberation Theology, took a long step toward that commitment in 1972 in the deliberations of its Commission on World Mission and Evangelism.

The Fifth Assembly of the WCC in Nairobi (1975) marks the beginning of the WCC's open commitment to the theology of liberation. The preparatory documents, written or approved by the WCC staff, spoke of "education for liberation," "structures of injustice and struggles for liberation" and the "common search of various faiths, cultures and ideologies." They insisted that Christians are now actively involved in the struggle for justice shoulder to shoulder with humanists, committed Marxists and others also dedicated to the liberation of humanity. They approvingly quote Gustavo Gutierrez in his affirmation that the Church must become "a place of liberation." The authors proclaim that "all of human history and all of secular history is leading towards Christ" and that He is behind the modern struggles for

justice in the world even if those involved in them
formally reject Him.

The WCC staff even quotes Joseph Needham in his
conclusion that "China is the only truly Christian country in the world in the present day, in spite of its absolute
rejection of all religion." Needham can say that because
he holds a "quality of life" view of salvation which says
that wherever good things are being done for people,
Christ is present, even though those doing those good
things may reject Him. Needham states that Christians
should support all revolutions against oppression and
that his own ideal is "a practical socialism, and in the
end, communism." It is apparent in the text that the
WCC authors of this document agree with Needham's
views at almost every point.

If there were any doubt as to their liberationist convictions, the section of the preparatory document entitled
"Structures of Injustice and Struggles for Liberation,"
makes the WCC staff's view very clear. They assert that
the hope of the gospel can be expressed only through
revolutionary struggle in situations of oppression. They
believe that the Exodus illustrates both the need for and
method of liberation for the oppressed of today. They
conclude that "the struggles for economic justice, political freedom and cultural renewal . . . [are] elements in
the total liberation of the world through the mission of
God." In this sense they opted for a secular view of
salvation in which political, economic and cultural liberation have been substituted for spiritual conversion
as the center of the mission of God in the world.

The summary statement of the WCC position on salvation clearly illustrates the shift in their theology from
conversion, forgiveness of sins, redemption and new
birth as central features of God's saving work toward a
man-centered view that sees salvation in terms of man's
struggle for liberation in every area of his life:

> Many Christians who for Christ's sake are involved in
> economic and political struggles against injustice and
> oppression ask themselves and the churches what it
> means today to be a Christian and a true church.

Without the salvation of the churches from their captivity in the interests of dominating classes, races and nations, there can be no liberating church for mankind... We seek the church which initiates actions for liberation and supports the work of other liberating groups without calculating self-interest... Within the comprehensive notion of salvation, we see the saving work in four social dimensions:
1. Salvation works in the struggle for economic justice against the exploitation of people by people.
2. Salvation works in the struggle for human dignity against political oppression by their fellow man.
3. Salvation works in the struggle for solidarity against the alienation of person from person.
4. Salvation works in the struggle of hope against despair in personal life.

While in 1968 the WCC was only beginning to feel its way toward some of the basic tenets of radical Liberation Theology, by 1975 this theology completely dominated the organization. Four key Protestant Latin American liberation theologians had assumed positions of leadership in the WCC by this time: Jose Miguez Bonino, Emilio Castro, Julio de Santa Ana and Rubem Alves. Their influence was felt throughout the organization. The theology they represented had quickly become the official position of the largest ecumenical organization in the world. The Fifth Assembly in 1975 saw the WCC leaders decide to attempt to spread the doctrines of radical Liberation Theology to all its member churches.

Since that time many conferences have been sponsored by the WCC in Latin America to teach these doctrines to Latin American Christian leaders. Many Latin American seminaries have received financial assistance from the WCC because of their support of radical Liberation Theology. At present the WCC is attempting to form a Latin American Council of Churches and recruit all of the Protestant denominations in Latin America as members. This would greatly increase their liberationist influence in this continent. They have become the primary promoter of radical Liberation Theology in the world, and their influence on the churches and seminaries of Latin America increases daily. The election of moderate liberationist Emilio Castro as the new leader of the WCC evidences their continuing commitment to this theology.

CHAPTER 10

What Does The Vatican Think About Liberation Theology?

The Roman Catholic Church has a long history of interest in social problems stemming back to 1891 when Pope Leo XIII published what has been called "the first social encyclical of the modern period," *Rerum Novarum.*[1] In this encyclical, according to Roman Catholic historian Jose Marins, "for the first time a pope expresses his thinking concerning the totality of the social problems of his day,"[2] urging Catholic laymen and clergy to become involved in the construction of a better society. In 1899 Pope Leo XIII convoked the first Latin American Plenary Council in Rome. That Council discussed the many threats to the Roman Catholic faith in Latin America, including paganism, superstition, socialism and freemasonry.[3] Perhaps the most important feature of the Council was that it allowed the bishops of Latin America to meet together to consider common problems and goals. Many new developments in Latin American theology have come from meetings among bishops that followed this 1899 beginning.

By 1912, as a result of the impetus of Pope Leo XIII's

social conscience, the Confederation of Catholic Workers' Circles was founded to encourage Catholic laymen to work for better conditions in their nations. From that beginning came what Andrew Kirk refers to as "the three most significant efforts at mobilizing the Church to face the challenge of mission in modern Latin America": the Catholic Action Movement, the Catholic Trade Union Movement and the Christian Democrat Party.[4] In these organizations, Catholic laypeople and clergy began to apply the social principles taught by the Roman Catholic Church to the work of labor unions, political parties, cooperatives, self-help programs and social services.[5]

Thinking back on this period, activist Brazilian bishop Helder Camara calls Catholic Action "our seminary, our noviciate. It trained some of our best militants. It prepared the way for the Council" (that is, the Vatican II Council).[6] Camara says that the great blessing of these movements was that they took priests and bishops out of their ecclesiastical isolation and placed them "right into the midst of the workers, peasants, students" where they saw the reality of social oppression and exploitation firsthand.[7]

Although the establishment of these social help movements was seen as the best way to stop Marxism from taking over the Latin American continent, the effect was to open clergy and laypeople's eyes to the suffering of the poor and the injustices being perpetrated by the rich and powerful against them.[8] When the bishops of Latin America met in Medellin in 1968, the lessons they learned in contact with the poor were translated into social analysis and plans for action.

In the 1930s and 1940s many Latin American priests and bishops traveled extensively in Europe, absorbing the radical concepts of social analysis in vogue there at that time.[9] Many returned to Latin America with the beginnings of what liberationist historian Enrique Dussel calls "scientific and theological reflection on the Latin American reality."[10] This "awakening" to the unique social problems of Latin America inspired the creation of "Centers for Social Investigation" all over Latin America.[11] Much of the preliminary thought behind radical Liberation Theology was worked out in those Centers.

Dussel concludes that by the beginning of the 1960s the Catholic Church had begun to experience dramatic changes which were crucial for the development of the Liberation Theology movement. The persecution of the church by some Latin American governments had cut the church's ties to the state and caused many Latin Americans to see the church as a possible ally against unjust government authorities. Also, the activity of the church in labor unions, Catholic Action and other social help programs had awakened many church leaders to the seriousness of the social plight of the poor. Finally, the injection of new theological, liturgical, catechetical and sociological concepts into the Latin American Roman Catholic Church had begun an intellectual ferment that was both hopeful and searching.[12]

How was the Vatican reacting to all of this change in the Latin American branch of the church? There is no doubt that the single most important factor in confirming and encouraging this wave of change was the Second Vatican Council (1962 - 1965).[13] More than 600 Latin American bishops were present at the Council meetings and they profited greatly from dialogue with other Third World bishops, studying in the Vatican's excellent research facilities and meeting with leaders like Father Gauthier, who challenged them with his concept of "a Church for the poor."[14]

The Vatican published *Guadium et Spes* as part of the official declarations of Vatican II. It depicts the problem of developing countries as one in which increasing poverty is directly related to their dependence on wealthier nations. It then calls for a "new humanism" in which men are responsible for their brothers.[15]

Populorum Progressio, the papal encyclical published after the Vatican II meetings, was much more direct and confrontational in its denunciation of social evils than *Gaudium et Spes* had been. As Gustavo Gutierrez observes, "it energetically denounces the international imperialism of money, situations whose injustice cries to heaven and the growing gap between rich and poor countries" and expresses the vision of mankind freed from all forms of servitude.[16] Gutierrez is somewhat critical of *Populorum Progressio* because it is "reformist" rather than "revolutionary." That is, it does not encourage revolt on the part of the suffering masses, but as Gutierrez affirms, it "addresses itself to the great ones of this world urging them to carry out the necessary changes."[17] Gutierrez sees it as a "transitional document" which, with its open opposition to unjust social structures, paved the way for the radicalization of the Latin Church from a reformist to a revolutionary posture.[18]

In 1968 the bishops of Latin America decided to meet together to apply the principles of Vatican II to their own Latin American situation.[19] The convocation, the CELAM II Meetings (General Council of the Latin American Episcopate), was held in Medellin, Colombia, in August of that year.[20] Prior to the CELAM meetings documents published by 17 Third World bishops and the provincial fathers of the Latin American Society of Jesus (the Jesuits) set the stage for a critical, penetrating analysis of the social problems of Latin America. This pressure on the church to commit itself to radical social change began to cause serious internal tensions in the Latin American Roman Catholic Church. Just before the CELAM meetings opened, the Brazilian newspaper, *O Jornal*, published a private document prepared by a group of Roman Catholic theologians under the leadership of Jose Comblin to be used by Bishop Helder Camara at the CELAM meetings. The newspaper accused Comblin of being a "Leninist theologian," and other Roman Catholic leaders announced that the document proved that "the communists have infiltrated the ecclesiastical hierarchy."[21]

The CELAM meetings followed right after the International Eucharistic Congress held in Bogota, Colombia. Pope Paul VI spoke to the priests there reminding them to have "intelligence and the courage of the Spirit in order to promote social justice, to love and defend the Poor."[22] Three days later, the Pope spoke to peasants urging them, "do not put your confidence in violence nor in revolution."[23] When the Pope opened the CELAM II meetings in Medellin on August 24, he reminded them that when theologians leave the traditional teaching of the Church, "they create in the area of faith a spirit of subversive criticism," but he also observed that "injustice is the first violence, the number one violence."[24] These mixed signals left the door wide open for many interpretations of the papal will when CELAM II began.

The documents produced by the CELAM II meetings shook the Catholic world with their radical appraisal of the Latin American situation of poverty, injustice and oppression. They announced that all "indicates that we are at the threshold of a new historical epoch in our continent, full of desire for a total emancipation, for liberation from all servitude."[25] They declared the bishops' conclusion that a new theology called the "theology of liberation" was the best vehicle for their pastoral concern and activist proposals for Latin America.[26] The documents contained lengthy condemnations of: the oppressive use of power, neo-colonialism, international monopolies, the international imperialism of money, injustice and institutionalized violence.[27] This combination of the social teaching of the church, the early church fathers and Scripture with Latin American Marxist analysis marks the first official use of Liberation Theology in the Roman Catholic Church and has caused many to see the CELAM II as the most significant event in the recent history of Latin American Roman Catholicism.[28]

The debate over Liberation Theology has become the central issue of Latin American Roman Catholicism since the CELAM II meetings in Medellin. That debate has become increasingly polarized and volatile as each side has become more supportive or more critical of Liberation Theology. The election of John Paul II to the papacy has meant an especially critical period in this ongoing conflict. Having suffered the effects of Marxist domination of his Polish homeland, John Paul II is no friend of Marxism and its religious counterpart, radical Liberation Theology.

As the debate waxed more and more heatedly, the liberationist leaders in the church hoped to recover a strong commitment from the leaders of the Latin American Church in the CELAM III meetings to be held in 1979 in Puebla, Mexico. By that time, however, Archbishop Alfonso Lopez Trujillo of Medellin, Colombia, (an avowed enemy of Liberation Theology) had become the leader of CELAM.[29] The opening remarks of Pope John Paul II set the tone for the entire Council. He called on the group of bishops and their elected representatives to "take Medellin's conclusions as its point of departure, with all the positive elements contained therein, but without disregarding the incorrect interpretations that have sometimes resulted and that call for calm discernment, opportune criticism, and clear-cut stances."[30] He also spoke out clearly against: "human, rational truth;" speculative re-readings of the gospel; political and revolutionary interpretations of Jesus; secularist interpretations of the kingdom of God which advocate bringing in the kingdom through "structural change and sociopolitical involvement;" the idea of a "people's Church;" "ideological polarization;" the reduction of truth to "mere political activity;" contamination of the church by modern humanism; "recourse to ideological systems in order to love, defend and collaborate in the liberation of the human being;" the assumption that all liberation is Christian; and clerics usurping the role of the laity in political and economic activities.[31]

The pope's condemnation of many of the controversial elements of radical Liberation Theology was a crushing blow to the liberationists, who attributed it to the behind-the-scenes influence of Archbishop Lopez Trujillo.[32] However the delegates to CELAM III followed Pope John Paul II's lead and in their final Council documents condemned secularism, Marxism, ideologies and violent revolution. In a statement that appears to be

a direct repudiation of radical Liberation Theology,
they concluded:

> We must also note the risk of ideologization run by
> theological reflection when it is based on a praxis that
> has recourse to Marxist analysis. The consequences
> are the total politicization of Christian experience, the
> disintegration of the language of faith into that of the
> social sciences, and the draining away of the tran-
> scendental dimension of Christian salvation.[33]

Liberation theologians such as Jon Sobrino, Gustavo
Gutierrez and Segundo Galilea have insisted that these
"criticisms of Liberation Theology" only reflect biased
interpretations of Puebla, since for them the CELAM III
conclusions reaffirm Medellin. This is not true however.[34] The CELAM III in Puebla was a clear call to
separate the church from Marxist ideology and bring it
back to the social teachings and strategies of the
church. It marks an authoritative and strategic rejection of many elements of radical Liberation Theology
from within the Latin American Roman Catholic
Church.

Pope John Paul II seemed to believe that this patent
rejection of radical Liberation Theology at Puebla would
stop the liberationist movement in the Latin American
Roman Catholic Church, but it has not. Increasing
numbers of Latin American Catholic theologians are
espousing radical Liberation Theology, and they are
being given more and more platforms from which to
publicly announce their views. In an effort to correct
this problem, the Vatican's Congregation for the Doctrine of the Faith (the doctrinal "watchdogs" of the
Roman Catholic Church) carried out an extensive study
in order to write a definitive Vatican statement on Liberation Theology under the guidance of Cardinal Joseph
Ratzinger, Vatican prefect and a leading expert on Liberation Theology. The documents they have published,
with the full approval of Pope John Paul II, have dealt a
devastating blow to the radical Liberation Theology
movement.

The first document, entitled "Instruction Concerning

Certain Aspects of the Theology of Liberation," was published in August of 1984 and centers heavily on a point-by-point criticism of radical Liberation Theology, which the authors refer to as "a perversion of the Christian message" (p. 28). The document admits that there are more moderate forms of this theology but condemns radical Liberation Theology for its "uncritical borrowings from Marxist ideology,"[35] "affirmation of necessary violence" for revolution[36] and use of "the most radical theses of rationalistic exegesis."[37] These three principal criticisms of radical Liberation Theology correspond to the problems we have already noted: it is Marxist, it is violent and it does away with the authority of God's Word. Following is a summary of the document's specific criticisms under those three headings.

A. It is Marxist:
1. The purpose of the document is to "attract the attention of pastors, of theologians and of the faithful, regarding the deviations and risks of deviation, which are ruinous for the faith and Christian life, that result from certain forms of the theology of liberation which utilize, in an insufficiently critical way, certain concepts taken from diverse strands of Marxist thought" (p. 4).
2. Radical Liberation Theology borrows concepts and methods from Marxism without making a critical analysis of whether or not they are compatible with the Christian faith (p. 20).
3. Radical Liberation Theology is an impatient movement which, in its rush to solve the critical social problems of Latin America, has accepted Marxist analysis of social reality with an almost mythical belief in Marxism's "scientific" realism and without critically examining its epistemological foundations (that is, the basis upon which it decides what is true, p. 21).
4. Marxism's oversimplified view of reality (its "ideology") is accepted by radical liberation theologians without understanding that reality is much more complicated than the Marxist analysis depicts it to be and must be understood much more deeply than Marxism

has been able to do (pp. 21-22).

5. It is a mistake, according to Pope Paul VI, to accept Marxist ideology and the theory of class struggle without "recognizing the kind of totalitarian society to which this process leads" (p. 22).

6. The Marxist idea of class struggle is unacceptable to Christians because it is "not compatible with the Christian concept of man and society" (p. 23).

7. Atheism and denial of individual worth are at the heart of Marxism and cause any theology linked with it to acquiesce to its "disregard for the spiritual nature of the person [which] leads to subordinating the person totally to the collectivity and, therefore, to denying the principles of social and political life in accord with human dignity" (p. 23).

8. Theology can never accept the conclusions of the social sciences regarding man and society without evaluating them "in the light of the Christian faith and what the faith teaches us regarding the truth about man and the ultimate meaning of his destiny" (p. 24).

9. Marxist dogma has convinced radical liberation theologians that only those who are involved in revolutionary praxis have the truth because they are "doing truth." This position denies all standards for ethics, morality and discernment of right and wrong outside the ranks of revolutionaries and their living out of the truth through insurrection. It is obvious that this view of an "inside" truth condemns radical Liberation Theology to listen to nothing but the echo of its own a priori revolutionary commitment (pp. 26-27).

10. Radical Liberation Theology sees class struggle as the "motor of history" in which "God becomes history" and the kingdom of God is identified with human liberation. "This identification stands in opposition to the faith of the Church" (pp. 28-29).

11. Instead of proclaiming the Christian virtue of universal love for all, radical Liberation Theology follows the logic of Marxist class struggle theory, seeing the rich person only as "a class enemy who must be fought" (pp. 29-30).

12. "Class struggle as the path leading to a society without classes is a myth which impedes reforms and worsens [the situation of] misery and injustice. Those who allow themselves to be captivated by this myth should reflect on the bitter historical experiences to which it has led" (p. 40).

13. Radical liberationists who use the Scriptures often attempt to make the biblical concept of the poor identical to Marx's concept of the "proletariat." So *"the Church of the poor* means in this sense a Church of class, that has become conscious of the need for revolutionary struggle as a step toward liberation and that celebrates this liberation in its liturgy" (pp. 30-31).

B. It is violent:

1. In radical Liberation Theology the legitimate cry of the poor and oppressed for justice has been perverted into a cry for "systematic recourse to violence" as the only way to solve their problems. This idea is unacceptable to Christians (p. 8).

2. The liberationist argument favoring the use of violence to reach the noble goals of well-being and justice for the oppressed poor destroys any concept of political morality or ethics, insisting that the end justifies the means (p. 27).

3. Radical Liberation Theology eliminates any possibility of going to rich oppressors through "the paths of non-violent dialogue and persuasion" and expecting them to change. It can only see them as enemies who must be destroyed (pp. 29-30).

4. Marxists do not abandon their use of violence after the "liberation" of the people but use it arbitrarily and unjustly against the very people they have "liberated" to maintain "the disgrace of our time: pretending to support liberty, whole nations are maintained in conditions of slavery unworthy of [any] man. Those who become accomplices of such slavery, perhaps unconsciously, betray the poor they intend to serve" (pp. 39-40).

C. It destroys the authority of God's Word:

1. "The meaning of this encounter [between modern man's aspiration for liberation and a true 'theology of liberation'] can be understood correctly only in the light of the specificity of the message of Revelation authentically interpreted by the Magisterium of the Church" (p. 9).

2. Radical Liberation Theology opposes the foundational teaching of the Old and New Testaments for human conduct: God's universal demand for brotherly love (pp. 12-13 and 29-30).

3. This theology reduces the gospel "to a purely earthly gospel" by affirming that "the struggle for human justice and liberty, understood in their economic and political sense, constitutes the essence and totality of salvation" (p. 19).

4. In radical Liberation Theology Marxist social analysis rather than divine revelation has become "the determining principle" for theology (p. 25).

5. The "new hermeneutic" of the theology of liberation "leads to an essentially political reading of the Scripture" which reduces the meaning of the biblical text to the political dimension (pp. 33-34).

6. The liberationists have accepted "the most radical theses of rationalistic exegesis ... [adopting] the opposition between the *'Jesus of history'* and the *'Jesus of faith'*" (p. 34).[38]

7. This theology "gives an exclusively political interpretation of the death of Christ" which "denies its salvific value and all the plan of redemption" (p. 35).

The document also contains some very helpful indications of the Christian alternative to radical Liberation Theology, stressing an active, effective ministry to meet the needs of the poor and faithfulness to the teaching of the church. Although it contains some appeals to the authority of the Magisterium (that is, the authoritative teaching office) of the Roman Catholic Church which are unacceptable to evangelicals, this document must still be recognized as one of the most comprehensive and

critically evaluative discussions of radical Liberation
Theology that has been published to date. The document ends with the words of Pope Paul VI: "We confess
that the Kingdom of God initiated here below in the
Church of Christ is not of this world, whose form passes
away, and that its proper growth cannot be confused
with the progress of civilization, of science or of human
technology" (p. 44). Archbishop Ratzinger also makes it
clear that Pope John Paul II has personally "approved
this Instruction" (p. 44).

That 1984 document promised a second publication
that would clearly point out the Christian doctrine of
"Christian liberty and liberation" (p. 4). It finally
appeared in March, 1986 under the title "Instruction on
Christian Liberty and Liberation."[39] This document
stresses heavily that spiritual redemption is the most
profound form of liberation (p. 4). The document argues
that the work of redemption from sin in Christ is the
center of the Christian message and therefore all reflection on liberation must begin there and be carried on in
the light of that truth (p. 4). The document traces the
history of humanity's search for liberty and offers a
number of philosophical and theological arguments
against tyranny, injustice and oppression. In spite of all
of its arguments against the use of violence and revolutionary uprisings, the most noted section of the document is entitled "A last recourse." In it the Vatican
Congregation opens the door to armed revolt as a last
recourse to put an end to an "evident and prolonged
tyranny that gravely imperils the fundamental rights of
the person and dangerously harms the common good of
the country" (p. 18). This position is entirely in keeping
with traditional Roman Catholic doctrine. Although the
Instruction hastens to add that armed revolt should be
considered only after "a very rigorous analysis of the
situation" and that "passive resistance" offers a more
moral and promising path to change, few Latin American Catholics seem to have read beyond the "last
recourse" statement. The conclusion splashed on the
front pages of many Latin American newspapers was

"Vatican justifies revolution!" Many Catholic leaders believe that this effect of the Instruction may well move the Congregation for the Doctrine of Faith to publish a further statement clarifying this point. Meanwhile the Latin American Roman Catholic Church continues down the road of increasing polarization and conflict. No one knows if this conflict may finally end in a division comparable only to the Protestant Reformation. In that kind of split liberationist Catholics might actually separate from the authority of the church, forming a competing "People's Church" founded on a federation of the continent's "base communities" where radical liberationist Biblical interpretation and active social involvement combine to make the "Church of the poor" a reality.[40]

Chapter 10, Notes

1. Andrew Kirk, *Liberation Theology*, p. 14.
2. Jose Marins y Equipo, *Praxis de los Padres de America Latina* (Bogota: Ediciones Paulinas, 1978), p. 21.
3. Enrique Dussel, *Historia de la Iglesia en America Latina*, p. 175.
4. Kirk, *Liberation Theology*, p. 15.
5. Dussel, *Historia de la Iglesia en America Latina*, pp. 181-182.
6. Jose de Broucker, *Dom Helder Camara: The Conversions of a Bishop* (New York: Collins, 1979), p. 120.
7. *Ibid.*, pp. 114-120.
8. Dussel, *Historia de la Iglesia en America Latina*, pp. 181-182.
9. *Ibid.*, p. 185
10. *Ibid.*
11. *Ibid.*, p. 186.
12. *Ibid.*, pp. 181-201.
13. Jose Marins, *Praxis de los Padres de America Latina*, p. 24; Dussel, *Historia de la Iglesia en America Latina*, p. 223; Jose de Broucker, *Dom Helder Camara: The Conversion of a Bishop*, p. 86.
14. Marins, *Praxis de los Padres de America Latina*, p. 24.
15. Gutierrez, *A Theology of Liberation*, pp. 33-34.
16. *Ibid.*, p. 34.
17. *Ibid.*
18. *Ibid.*
19. Dussel, *Historia de la Iglesia en America Latina*, p. 230.
20. "CELAM" is the acronym for the "General Council of the Latin American Episcopate," and was founded in 1955.
21. Dussel, *Historia de la Iglesia en America Latina*, p. 228.
22. *Ibid.*, p. 229.
23. *Ibid.*

24. *Ibid.*, p. 230.
25. *Ibid.*, p. 231.
26. *Ibid.* This section of the document reflects the thinking of Gustavo Gutierrez, who was deeply influenced by the Protestant theologian, Rubem Alves, years before the CELAM II.
27. Dussel, *Historia de la Iglesia en America Latina*, p. 231 (and corroborated in the actual texts of the CELAM II meetings).
28. Dussel, *Historia de la Iglesia en America Latina*, p. 233; Kirk, *Liberation Theology*, pp. 27-28; "Declaration of Golconda," as quoted in a document of the World Council of Churches' Latin American Department in their meeting July 24-26, 1969, in Geneva, Switzerland.
29. See Alfonso Lopez Trujillo, *Liberacion o Revolucion?* (Bogota: Ediciones Paulinas, 1975).
30. *Puebla* (London: Billing & Sons, 1980), p. 1.
31. *Puebla*, pp. 2-13.
32. See Jon Sobrino, *Puebla: serena afirmacion de Medellin* (Bogota: Indo-American Press, 1979), pp. 13-17.
33. *Puebla*, p. 114.
34. See, Sobrino, *Puebla: serena afirmacion de Medellin;* Gutierrez, *Los Padres y la liberacion en Puebla* (Bogota: Indo-American Press, 1979); and Galilea, *Teologia de la liberacion despues de Puebla* (Bogota: Indo-American Press, 1979).
35. "Instruccion sobre algunos aspectos de la Teologia de la Liberracion" (Medellin: Libreria del Seminario, 1984), p. 20. I will be translating directly from the Spanish version of the document in order to show more exactly the way in which this document has come to Latin America. Page numbers in parentheses correspond to this version of the "Instruction."
36. *Ibid.*, p. 27.
37. *Ibid.*, p. 34.
38. The dichotomy which has been created between the "Jesus of history" and the "Christ of faith" has become very popular in much of modern theology. According to this view, the writers of the New Testament created a "Christ of faith" after Jesus' death by adding myths, fables, embellishments and legends to the historical facts about Jesus. In its most radical form, this view declares that everything supernatural in the text of the New Testament is invention and that the "Jesus of history" was just an ordinary man with some extraordinary teaching. Much of what has been called "the quest for the historical Jesus" has been a series of attempts by various theologians to strip away the inventions and imaginings "of faith" and get back to the real facts about Jesus. Evangelical theologians reject this perspective, believing that there is no contradiction between the "Jesus of history" and the "Christ of faith"—they are one and the same, supernatural Son of God. For an interesting discussion of the liberal view, see Albert Schwietzer's *The Quest of the Historical Jesus* (London: A. C. Black, 1911).
39. Again, I will be translating directly from the Spanish version of the document "Instruccion sobre Libertad Cristiana y Liberacion"

as it appeared in "Documentos," *El Mundo*, Medellin, Colombia, April 24, 1986. Page numbers in parentheses correspond to this version of the "Instruction."

40. See, for example, A. William Cook, "The Expectation of the Poor: A Protestant Missiological Study of the Catholic 'Comunidades de Base' in Brazil," an excellent doctoral dissertation for the School of World Mission of Fuller Theological Seminary, 1982, pp. 201-212, 484-496; Leonardo Boff, "Theological Characteristics of a Grassroots Church," in Sergio Torres and John Eagleson (eds.), *The Challenge of Basic Christian Communities* (Maryknoll: Orbis Books, 1981), pp. 124-144; Jose Miguez Bonino, "Fundamental Questions in Ecclesiology," pp. 145-149 of the same work; Leonardo Boff, *Church, Charism and Power: Liberation Theology and the Institutional Church* (NY: Crossroad, 1985).

CHAPTER 11

What About Latin American Evangelicals And Liberation Theology?

Although Liberation Theology was first born in Latin America among Protestant theologians and then among Roman Catholics, it has found a very mixed reception among Latin American evangelicals. Some have rejected it totally; others have accepted it with certain internal conflicts; others have analyzed it, retaining the positive and criticizing the negative.

The Biblical Seminary of Colombia, where I teach, fits in the third category. We have studied radical Liberation Theology in some depth and encourage our students to study it as well. We have discovered several positive elements in Liberation Theology. For example, the liberation theologians are very critical of traditional theology. Their criticism has provided us with ample opportunities for self-analysis. As we have already pointed out, they criticize traditional theology's tendency to incorporate elements of Greek philosophy in the interpretation of the Scriptures and to overemphasize doctrinal orthodoxy and ignore the importance of "orthopraxis" (right actions). They have also charged that missionaries from the United States and Europe have mixed the gospel message they brought to Latin America with their own cultural, political and ideological convictions.

This kind of corrective is always beneficial and has helped us re-evaluate our presentation of the gospel to make sure it conforms more to the Scriptures and less to our own cultural and ideological patterns. The liberation theologians have also helped us to see the poverty, exploitation, oppression and misery of Latin America with more understanding, compassion and concern. Through their own interpretive excesses, they have forced us to define more exactly our beliefs regarding the relationship between the Old and New Testaments, especially in terms of their relative value for theology (the liberationists use the two testaments indiscriminately). Finally, radical Liberation Theology has caused evangelicals all over Latin America to analyze, evaluate and correct the lack of social ministry in our churches. All of this self-evaluation is valuable.

We have also found serious weaknesses in the radical Liberation Theology movement. The fundamental problem with this theology is its destruction of the normativity of biblical truth for Christian faith and practice. Many of the liberationists have substituted Marxism, or at least revolutionary action (praxis), for the Scriptures as the basis for theology. As evangelicals, we can never accept this substitution. It can only lead to theological chaos and confusion. We have also had to reject the "reductionism" of radical Liberation Theology, which often reduces the Christian faith to little more than revolutionary political action. Finally, as evangelicals we have had to declare ourselves in opposition to the implicit universalism that stands behind much of the rhetoric of this theology. If all men were saved regardless of what they do about Jesus Christ, we could agree with the liberationists that evangelism is a waste of time and dedicate ourselves completely to bettering the lives of the poor of Latin America. But such is not the case. People's eternal destinies will be determined by the decision they make in this life concerning Jesus Christ and His Word. We cannot, we will not deny the biblical priority on evangelism accompanied by compassionate social ministry.

The study of radical Liberation Theology has enriched our seminary and the students from various Latin American countries who attend it. Recently a student shared about a young couple who had given their lives to Christ after the morning service one Sunday. I was pleased to hear of their conversion, but I was also pleased to hear the way in which Nicanor, the student, had found out that they were in desperate economic straits. He had immediately begun to look for a job for the young husband (he found one), while Nicanor's wife began teaching the young wife how to make Christmas decorations to supplement their meager income. That might not have happened here 10 years ago, but I praise the Lord that it is a common occurrence now. Our students are committed to an integral ministry with a priority on evangelism and a practical compassion that helps meet the needs of the total person. That has been one of the positive effects of our study of radical Liberation Theology. We have repudiated its errors, listened to its criticisms and changed our ways as we have seen new light on a fuller obedience to the total message of the gospel. In spite of its heresies and distortions, radical Liberation Theology has awakened us, perhaps through our correction of its extremes, to a fuller responsiveness to the message of Christ.

Some evangelical leaders and institutions in Latin America have rejected everything in radical Liberation Theology because of their belief that any teaching having anything to do with Marxism is "of the devil." These people are apt to equate true Christianity with "the American way" and democratic capitalism. Most of them are United States missionaries, who see the Christian faith as an extension of the ideals of American culture, economics and politics, or their Latin American disciples, who unwittingly adopt their attitudes without understanding the foreign origin of their convictions.

They add fuel to the fire of the liberationist charges of "religious imperialism."

Christianity cannot be reduced to an ideological option—capitalism or Marxism. It cannot be equated with any man-made system. Our faith judges all systems, ideologies and political theories without aligning itself with any. There is a qualitative difference between the kingdom of God and human kingdoms.

Other evangelicals have accepted radical Liberation Theology with certain internal conflicts, since it is virtually impossible to reconcile genuine evangelical faith with the rejection of Biblical authority, substitution of Marxism for the authoritative teaching of God's Word, reductionism and the universalism of the radical liberation theologians. Sadly, many Latin American seminaries that were once bastions of evangelical doctrine have been drifting for years towards a less-than-authoritative view of Scripture which has left them open for the enticements and attacks of radical Liberation Theology. Many have now capitulated completely and have become some of the most prolific promoters of radical Liberation Theology in Latin America. Many of the evangelical churches pastored by liberationists have become little more than centers for social action and revolutionary indoctrination. In many cases, as the members of the churches have come to realize that a "new gospel" is being preached to them, they have abandoned their churches and left behind a small, radical group deeply committed to the pastor and his new doctrine. These pastors, who are often extremely vocal and well-prepared theologically, are deeply involved in ministerial associations and denominational leadership in order to move more and more organizations toward a liberationist commitment. They are very successful in many cases and have been able to paralyze or at least cripple foreign missionary involvement in many associations, denominations and local churches.

Latin American evangelicals must not refuse the gauntlet that the liberation theologians have thrown down, but they must pick it up and answer their challenge point by point. Many of us believe that God is calling us as national Christians and foreign missionaries to "contend for the faith" as never before in the history of this continent. Radical Liberation Theology could easily destroy much of the fruit of 100 years of missionary and national church work in Latin America unless it is stopped by well-prepared spokesmen for biblical truth. With more than 80 percent of the pastors in Latin America having no formal theological education whatsoever, the few seminaries and Bible institutes in the continent must do all they can to prepare as many leaders as possible who are equipped with a reasonable faith and a contagious spiritual fervor. These leaders must not only stand against the attacks of radical Liberation Theology but they must also offer a biblical alternative for integral ministry.

Latin American theologians who can think for themselves and deal with the proponents of radical Liberation Theology on their own academic level must be trained. We have already seen a case in which Protestant and Roman Catholic liberationists banded together in Nicaragua to support a successful revolution and the establishment of a socialist society. They are attempting to carry out the same program in El Salvador right now. More than 10 years ago they devised sophisticated plans for bringing about similar revolutions in every country of Latin America during the "Christians for Socialism" Encounter in Santiago, Chile. They are now carrying out those plans, and they have been very successful in their efforts. Unless something is done soon to stem this tide of theological subversion, the Latin American Church is doomed to become a mere appendage to the Marxist revolutionary movement, which is more than willing to discard its "appendages" after it has reached its goals. (This can be seen in Nicaragua already.)

Those of us who stand on the edge of this coming destruction, both missionaries and national leaders, ask for your prayers that the Lord will grant us wisdom, humility and courage to face the days that await us.

There may not be much time left for missionary influence on this continent. We must make every day count for the multiplication of godly, well-equipped Latin American leaders.

We must respond to the challenge of radical Liberation Theology with the humility born of the realization that although God's Word is perfect, our interpretations of it are not. We must be willing to learn from others, but we must also be willing to stand for what we know is true. We are not fighting for "traditional theology" but for the "faith once delivered to the saints." If our battle with radical Liberation Theology has helped us to see God's truth more clearly, analyze our own lives more critically, commit ourselves to evangelism more unreservedly, care for people's physical needs more compassionately, hold to the authority of God's Word more tenaciously and live His truths more effectively, then in spite of all of its errors and extremes, radical Liberation Theology will have served us well.

English Language Bibliography

Albrecht, Paul. *The Churches and Rapid Social Change*. Garden City: Doubleday, 1961.

Alves, Rubem. "Christian Realism: Ideology of the Establishment," *Christianity and Crisis* (September 17, 1973), pp. 173-176.

—————. "Confessions: On Theology and Life," *Union Seminary Quarterly* XXIX:3/4 (1974), pp. 181-193; published later as "From Paradise to the Desert: Autobiographical Musings," in Rosino Gibellini (ed.), *Frontiers of Theology in Latin America,* London: SCM Press, 1980, pp. 284-303.

—————. "The Crisis in the Congregatrion," *International Review of Mission* LX:237 (1971).

—————. "Giving Account of Faith: Political and Social Implications—Where Is the Church?", *Study Encounter 77* XI:2 (1975), pp. 1-3.

—————. "The Hermeneutics of the Symbol," *Theology Today* XXIX:1 (1972), pp. 46-53.

—————. *I Believe in the Resurrection of the Body*. Philadelphia: Fortress, 1986.

—————. "Identity and Communication," *WACC Journal* XXII:4, pp. 6-10.

—————. Is There Any Future for Protestantism in Latin America?", *The Lutheran Quarterly* XXII:1, pp. 49-59.

—————. "The Life of the Churches and the Ecumenical Movement in Latin America," *Reformed and Presbyterian World* XXXI:2 (1970), pp. 5-27.

—————. "Marxism as the Guarantee of Faith," *Worldview* (March 1973), pp. 13-17.

—————. "Personal Wholeness and Political Creativity: The Theology of Liberation and Pastoral Care," *Pastoral Psychology* 26 (1977), pp. 124-136.

—————. "Priorities for Peace in Inter-American Relations," *World Christian Education* (1967), pp. 40-44.

—————. *Protestantism and Repression: A Brazilian Case Study*. Maryknoll: Orbis Books, 1985.

—————. "Protestantism in Latin America: Its Ideological Function and Utopian Possibilities," *Ecumenical Review* 22 (1970), pp. 1-15.

—————. "Religion: Pathology or Search for Sanity," *Encounter* XXXVI:1 (1975), pp. 1-9.

—————. *A Theology of Human Hope*. Washington: Corpus, 1969.

Alves, Rubem. "Theology and the Liberation of Man," in SODEPAX, *In Search of a Theology of Development,* Geneva: Committee on Society, Development and Peace, 1970, pp. 75-92.

_____. "Theses for a Reconstruction of Theology," *Documents, IDOC—International North American Edition* (October 31, 1970), pp. 3-16.

_____. *Tomorrow's Child: Imagination, Creativity and the Rebirth of Culture.* New York: Harper and Row, 1972.

_____. "Utopia Becomes Ideology," in Jorge Lara-Braud (ed.), *Our Claim on the Future,* New York: Friendship Press, 1970, pp. 62-78.

_____. "Violence and Counterviolence," in Samuel Shapiro (ed.), *Cultural Factors in Inter-American Relations,* South Bend: Notre Dame Press, 1967.

_____. *What Is Religion?* Maryknoll: Orbis Books, 1984.

Amaya, Israel, "The Theology of Liberation," *Theological Fraternity Bulletin* 3 (1974), pp. 2-5.

Armerding, Carl (ed.). *Evangelicals and Liberation.* Phillipsburg, New Jersey: Presbyterian and Reformed Publishing, 1979.

Anderson, Gerald H. and Thomas F. Stransky (eds.). *Crucial Issues in Mission Today.* Grand Rapids: Eerdmans, 1974.

_____. *Liberation Theologies.* Grand Rapids: Eerdmans, 1979.

_____. *Third World Theologies.* Grand Rapids: Eerdmans, 1976.

Arias, Esther and Mortimer. *The Cry of My People.* New York: Friendship Press. 1980.

Arias, Mortimer. "The Church and Revolution," in IDOC, *Gospel and Violence: Bolivia,* Rome: IDOC, 1974.

_____. "Jesus Christ Frees and Unites," *One World* 4 (1975), pp. 16-17.

Assmann, Hugo. "The Christian Contribution to the Liberation of Latin America," *Anticipation* 9 (1971), pp. 14-27.

_____. "The Power of Christ in History: Conflicting Christologies and Discernment," in Rosino Gibellini (ed.), *Frontiers of Theology in Latin America.* London: SCM Press, 1980.

_____. *Practical Theology of Liberation.* London: Search Press, 1975 (also published as *Theology for a Nomad Church.* Maryknoll: Orbis Books, 1976).

_____. "Theological training and diversity of ministries," *International Review of Mission* 66 (1977), pp. 22-28.

Balasuriya, Tissa. *Jesus Christ and Human Liberation.* Colombo: Centre for Society and Religion, 1975.

Bammel, Ernst. "The revolution theory from Reimarus to Brandon," in E. Bammel and C. F. D. Moule (eds.), *Jesus and the Politics of His Day,* Cambridge: Cambridge University Press, 1984, pp. 11-68.

Banana, Canaan. "The Biblical basis for liberation struggles," *International Review of Mission* 68 (1979), pp. 417-423.

Banks, Robert. "A Christian Revolutionary Tradition?", *Journal of Ecumenical Studies* IV:2 (1972), pp. 285-300.

Barreno Barreno, Manuel Maria. *Conflicting Theologies Met at Puebla,* unpublished doctoral dissertation for the Aquinas Institute of Theology, 1982.

Beardslee, William A. "New Testament Perspectives on Revolution as a Theological Problem," *Journal of Religion* LI:1 (January, 1971), p. 19.

Benjamin, Walter W. "Liberation theology: European hopelessness exposes the Latin hoax; material plenty is always the Marxist promise, yet always deferred," *Christianity Today* 26 (March 5, 1982), pp. 21-23.

Berryman, Phillip E. "Latin American Liberation Theology," *Theological Studies* XXXIV:3 (1973), pp. 357-395.

Beyerhaus, Peter. "Theology of Salvation in Bangkok," *Christianity Today* XVII:13 (March 30, 1973), pp. 11-17.

Bianchi, Eugene C. *The Religious Experience of Revolutionaries*. Garden City: Doubleday, 1972.

Bigo, Pierre. *The Church and Third World Revolution*. Maryknoll: Orbis Books, 1977.

Blachnicki, Franciszek. "A theology of liberation—in the Spirit," *Religion in Communist Lands* 12 (Summer, 1984), pp. 157-167.

Bloch, Ernst. *Atheism in Christianity: The Religion of the Exodus and the Kingdom*. New York: Herder and Herder, 1972.

Bockmuehl, Klaus. *The Challenge of Marxism: A Christian Response*. Leicester: Inter-Varsity, 1980.

Boesak, Allan A. (ed.). *A Call for an end to unjust rule*. Edinburgh: Saint Andrews Press, 1986.

_____ . *Farewell to innocence: a social-ethical study of black theology and black power*. Johannesburg: Ravan Press, 1977.

_____ . *The Finger of God: sermons on faith and socio-political responsibility*. Maryknoll: Orbis Books, 1982.

_____ . *Walking on thorns: the call to Christian obedience*. Geneva: World Council of Churches, 1984.

_____ . "Wholeness through liberation," *Church and Society* 71 (May/June, 1981), pp. 31-39.

Boff, Leonardo. "Christ's Liberation via Oppression: An Attempt at Theological Construction from the Standpoint of Latin America," in Rosino Gibellini (ed.), *Frontiers of Theology in Latin America*, London: SCM Press, 1980.

_____ . *Church, Charism and Power: Liberation Theology and the Institutional Church*. New York: Crossroad, 1985.

_____ . *Ecclesiogenesis: the base communities reinvent the Church*. Maryknoll: Orbis Books, 1983.

_____ . *Jesus Christ Liberator: A Critical Christology of Our Time*. London: SPCK, 1980.

_____ . *Liberating Grace*. Maryknoll: Orbis Books, 1979.

_____ . *The Lord's Prayer: the prayer of integral liberation*. Maryknoll: Orbis Books, 1983.

_____ . *The People of God amidst the poor*. London: T and T Clark, 1984.

_____ . *Option for the poor: challenge to the rich countries*. London: T and T Clark, 1986.

_____ . *The Question of Faith in the Resurrection of Jesus*. Chicago:

Franciscan Herald Press, 1971.

Boff, Leonardo. *Saint Francis: a model for human liberation.* New York: Crossroads, 1982.

_____. *Way of the Cross—Way of Justice.* Maryknoll: Orbis Books, 1980.

Boff, Leonardo and Clodovis Boff. *Liberation Theology from Dialogue to Confrontation.* San Francisco: Harper Row, 1986.

_____. *Salvation and Liberation.* Maryknoll: Orbis Books, 1984.

Bonhoeffer, Dietrich. *Letters and Papers from Prison.* London: SCM Press, 1979.

Borman, John. *A Study in Christianity, Marxist Ideology and Historical Engagement with Special Reference to the Liberation Theology of Jose Miguez Bonino,* unpublished doctoral dissertation for the University of Cape Town, 1983.

Bosch, David J. "Contextual missionary theology from Orbis: a bold publishing venture," *Missionalia* XIII:3 (November, 1985), pp. 121-131.

Braaten, Carl E. "Praxis: the Trojan horse of liberation theology," *Dialog* 23 (Autumn, 1984), pp. 276-280.

_____. *History and Hermeneutics.* Philadelphia: Westminster Press, 1966.

Bracken, Joseph A. "Faith and Justice: A New Synthesis?—The Interface of Process and Liberation Theologies," *Process Studies* 14 (Summer, 1985), pp. 73-141.

Brandon, S. G. F. *Jesus and the Zealots: A Study of the Political Factor in Primitive Christianity.* Manchester: Manchester University Press, 1967.

Breneman, J. Mervin. "Some Notes on Continuity and/or Discontinuity between the Kingdom of God and History," *Theological Fraternity Bulletin* 4 (December, 1973), pp. 1-7.

_____. "The Use of the Exodus in Theology," *Theological Fraternity Bulletin* 3 (1974), pp. 5-9.

Broucker, Jose de. *Dom Helder Camara: The Conversion of a Bishop.* New York/London: Collins, 1979.

_____. *Dom Helder Camara: The Violence of a Peacemaker.* Maryknoll: Orbis Books, 1970.

Brown, Robert McAfee. "Drinking from our own wells," *The Christian Century* 101 (May 9, 1984), pp. 483-486.

_____. *Religion and Violence: A Primer for White Americans.* Philadelphia: Westminster Press, 1973.

_____. *Theology in a New Key: Responding to Liberation Themes.* Philadelphia: Westminster Press, 1978.

_____. *Unexpected news: reading the Bible with Third World eyes.* Philadelphia: Westminster Press, 1984.

Bundy, Edgar C. (ed.). *The Marxist-Revolutionary Invasion of the Latin American Churches.* Wheaton: Church League of America, 1972.

Cabestrero, Teolfilo. *Ministers of God, Ministers of the People: Testimonies of Faith from Nicaragua.* Maryknoll: Orbis Books, 1983.

Cabrera, Miguel A. "The church in Brazil: a church on the road to liberation," *Exchange* 12 (April, 1983), pp. 1-66.

Camara, Dom Helder. *Church and Colonialism.* London: Sheed and Ward, 1969.

———. *Race against Time.* London: Sheed and Ward, 1971.

———. *Revolution through Peace.* Evanston: Harper and Row, 1971.

———. *Spiral of Violence.* London: Sheed and Ward, 1971.

Cardenal, Ernesto. *Love in Practice: The Gospel in Solentiname.* London: Search Press, 1977.

Castillo Cardenas, Gonzalo. "The Challenge of the Latin American Revolution," in J. C. Bennett (ed.), *Christian Social Ethics in a Changing World,* New York, Association Press, 1966.

———. "From Protest to Revolutionary Commitment," *International Review of Mission* LX:238 (1971), pp. 212-222.

Castro, Emilio. *Amidst Revolution.* Belfast: Christian Journal Limited, 1975.

———. "Bangkok: The New Opportunity," *International Review of Mission* LXII:246 (1973), pp. 136-143.

———. "A Call to Action," in Thomas E. Quigley (ed.), *Freedom and Unfreedom in the Americas,* New York: IDOC, 1971.

———. "Christian Response to the Latin American Revolution," *Christianity and Crisis* XXIII:15 (1963), pp. 160-163.

———. "Conflict and Reconciliation," *Ecumenical Review* XXV:3 (1973), pp. 286-294.

———. "Conversion and Social Transformation," in J. C. Bennett (ed.), *Christian Social Ethics in a Changing World,* New York: Association Press, 1966, pp. 348-368.

———. "Ecumenical Relationships in Latin America," *Lutheran World* XV:4 (1968), pp. 271-278.

———. "End of the Siesta," *Frontier* 10 (1967/1968), pp. 269-272.

———. "Evangelism and Social Justice," *Ecumenical Review* XX:2 (1968), pp. 146-150.

———. "Evangelism in the Third World," *Review and Expositor* 74 (1977), pp. 149-158.

———. "Evangelization in Latin America," *International Review of Mission* LIII:212 (1964), pp. 452-456.

———. "First WCC Meeting in Portugal," *IDOC Bulletin* 28 (1975), pp. 3-7.

———. *Freedom in mission: the perspective of the Kingdom of God—an ecumenical inquiry.* Geneva: World Council of Churches, 1985.

———. "From the Editor," *International Review of Mission* LXIII:252 (1974), pp. 473-474.

———. "Ministry with the Poor," *International Review of Mission* 66 (1977), pp. 1-80.

———. "Mission in a World of Cities: A Panel Presentation," *Student World* 3 (1968), pp. 217-223.

———. "Mission Today," *Missiology: An International Review* XI:3 (1974), pp. 359-367.

———. "On Isaiah 55," in Hendrikus Berkhof and Philip Potter

(eds.), *Key Words of the Gospel,* London: SCM Press, 1964, pp. 116-126.

Castro, Emilio. "Pentecostalism and Ecumenism in Latin America," *Christian Century* 89 (1972), pp. 955-957.

————. "The Perspective of the Cross," *Study Encounter* 3 (1966), pp. 106-108.

————. "Salvation Today at Bangkok and After," *Study Encounter* 75 XI:2 (1975) pp. 4-11.

————. *Sent Free: unity in the perspective of the Kingdom.* Grand Rapids: Eerdmans, 1985.

————. "The World Council of Churches and liberationism," *The Christian Century* 102 (November 13, 1985), p. 1025.

Catherwood, Sir Frederick. *A Better Way: the case for a Christian social order.* Leicester: Inter-Varsity, 1976.

Chapman, G. Clarke, "Bonhoeffer: resource for liberation theology," *Union Seminary Quarterly Review* 36 (Summer, 1981), pp. 225-242.

Comblin, Jose. *The Church and the National Security State.* New York: Orbis Books, 1979.

Cone, James H. "Biblical Revelation and Social Existence," *Interpretation* XXVIII:4 (1974), pp. 422-440.

————. *Black Theology and Black Power.* New York: Harper and Row, 1969.

————. *A Black Theology of Liberation.* Philadelphia/NY: J. B. Lippincott, 1970.

————. *God of the Oppressed.* New York: Seabury, 1975.

————. "The gospel and the liberation of the poor: how my mind has changed," *The Christian Century* 98 (February 18, 1981), pp. 162-166.

————. *My Soul Looks Back.* Nashville: Abingdon, 1982.

————. *Speaking the Truth: Ecumenism, Liberation and Black Theology.* Grand Rapids: Eerdmans, 1986.

Conway, James F. *Marx and Jesus: Liberation Theology in Latin America.* New York: Carlton Press, 1973.

Cook, Michael L. "Jesus from the other side of history: Christology in Latin America," *Theological Studies* 44 (June, 1983), pp. 258-287.

Cook, William (Guillermo). "Base Ecclesial Community: A Protestant Perspective," *Transformation* III:3 (1986), pp. 5-6.

————. *The Expectation of the Poor: Latin American Base Ecclesial Communities in Protestant Perspective.* Maryknoll: Orbis Books, 1985.

Corbitt, Duvon C., Sr. *Liberation Theology.* Wilmore, KY: Asbury Press, 1981.

Costas, Orlando. *The Church and Its Mission: A Shattering Critique from the Third World.* Wheaton: Tyndale, 1974.

————. "Mission Out of Affluence," *Missiology: An International Review* I:4 (1973).

————. *Theology of the Crossroads in Contemporary Latin America: Missiology in Mainline Protestantism: 1969-1974.* Amsterdam: Rodopi, 1976.

Cox, Harvey (ed.). *The Church Amid Revolution.* New York: Association Press, 1967.

Croatto, Jose Severino. *Exodus: A Hermeneutic of Freedom.* Maryknoll: Orbis Books, 1981.

Dahl, Howard. *Praxis: A Ground for Truth?*, unpublished masters thesis for Trinity Evangelical Divinity School, 1977.

Davies, J. G. *Christians, Politics and Violent Revolution.* London: SCM Press, 1976.

Davis, Edmund. "Social and spiritual implications of a theology of liberation," *Caribbean Journal of Religious Studies* 5 (1983), pp. 43-51.

Desroches, Henry. *Christ the Liberator.* Bangalore: The Centre for Social Action, 1977.

Dewart, Leslie. *Christianity and Revolution: the Lesson of Cuba.* New York: Herder and Herder, 1963.

Dickinson, Richard D. *To Set at Liberty the Oppressed.* Geneva: WCC, 1975.

Dodson, Michael. "Liberation Theology and Christian Radicalism in Contemporary Latin America," *Journal of Latin American Studies,* 1979.

Dupertuis, Atilio R. "Liberation theology's use of the exodus as a soteriological model," *Andrews University Seminary Studies* 20 (Summer, 1982), pp. 151-152.

Dussel, Enrique. "Church-State Relations in Peripheral Latin American Formations," *The Ecumenical Review* 29 (1977), pp. 28-38.

————. *Ethics and the Theology of Liberation.* Maryknoll: Orbis Books, 1978.

————. *History and the Theology of Liberation.* Maryknoll: Orbis Books, 1976.

————. *Philosophy of Liberation.* Maryknoll: Orbis Books, 1985.

————. "The political and ecclesial context of liberation theology in Latin America," in Sergio Torres (ed.), *The Emergent Gospel: Theology from the Underside of History.* Maryknoll: Orbis Books, 1977.

Eagleson, John (ed.). *Christians and Socialism: Documentation of the Christians for Socialism Movement in Latin America.* Maryknoll: Orbis Books, 1975.

————. "Orbis books and liberation theology," *American Theological Library Association: Proceedings* 39 (1985), pp. 130-140.

Edwards, George R. *Jesus and the Politics of Violence.* New York: Harper and Row, 1972.

Eller, Vernard. "Onesimus: A Study in Ethics," *TSF Bulletin* VIII:4 (1985), pp. 10-13.

Elliott, Mark. "Thesis [list of dissertations on the church and religion in Communist countries]," *Religion in Communist Lands* 13 (1985), pp. 322-323.

Ellul, Jacques. *Autopsy of Revolution.* New York: Knopf, 1971.

————. *Money and Power.* Downers Grove: Inter-Varsity Press, 1984.

————. *The Subversion of Christianity.* Grand Rapids:

Eerdmans, 1986.

Ellul, Jacques. *Violence: Reflections from a Christian Perspective.* New York: Seabury, 1969, and London: SCM Press, 1970.

Eppstein, John. *The Cult of Revolution in the Church.* New York: Abingdon, 1974.

Escobar, Samuel. "Christian Base Communities: A Historical Perspective," *Transformation* III:3 (1986), pp. 1-4.

_____. "Evangelical faith and liberation theology," *Together* 7 (1985), pp. 18-21.

_____. "The Kingdom of God, Eschatology and Social and Political Ethics in Latin America," *Theological Fraternity Bulletin* 1 (1975), pp. 1-42.

_____ and others. "A Latin American critique of Latin American theology," *Evangelical Review of Theology* VII:1 (1983), pp. 48-62.

Escobar, Samuel and John Driver. *Christian Mission and Social Justice.* Scottsdale, PA: Herald Press, 1978.

Fabella, Virginia and Sergio Torres (eds.). *Doing theology in a divided world: papers from the Sixth International Conference of the Ecumenical Association of Third World Theologians, January 5-13, 1983, Geneva, Switzerland.* Maryknoll: Orbis Books, 1985.

Facelina, Raymond. *Liberation and Salvation: International Bibliography.* Strasbourg: CERDIC Publications, 1973.

Faleiro, Braz. "Mission of the church in India today: to preach and work for the liberation of the oppressed," *Religion and Society* XXXI:2 (1985), pp. 54-58.

Fals-Borda, Orlando. *Subversion and Social Change in Colombia.* New York: Columbia University Press, 1969.

Fierro, Alfredo. *The Militant Gospel: An Analysis of Contemporary Political Theologies.* London: SCM Press, 1977, and Maryknoll: Orbis Books, 1977.

Fiorenza, Francisco P. "Latin American Liberation Theology," *Interpretation* XXVIII (1974), pp. 441-445.

Foulkes, Ricardo. "Liberation in the Gospels," *Theological Fraternity Bulletin* 4 (1975), pp. 9-28.

Freire, Paulo. *Education for Critical Consciousness.* New York: Continuum, 1973.

_____. "Education, liberation and the church," *Religious Education* 79 (Fall, 1984), pp. 524-545.

_____. *Pedagogy of the Oppressed.* New York: Herder and Herder, 1970.

_____. *The Politics of Education: culture, power and liberation.* South Hadley, MA: Bergin and Garvey, 1984.

Gadorf, Christine Erhart. *Contested Issues in Twentieth Century Papal Teaching: The Position of the Vatican in Light of the Challenge from Liberation Theology,* unpublished doctoral dissertation for Columbia University, 1979.

Galiliea, Segundo. *The Beatitudes: To Evangelize as Jesus Did.* Maryknoll: Orbis Books, 1984.

Garcia, J.A. and Cr. Calle (eds.). *Camilo Torres: Priest and Revolu-*

tionary. London: Sheed and Ward, 1968.

Garcia, Jose Rafael. *Liberation and Evil: a critique of the thought of Gustavo Gutierrez and Rubem Alves from the standpoint of F. R. Tennant's theodicy,* unpublished doctoral dissertation for Claremont Graduate School, 1975.

Gauthier, Paul. *Christ, the Church and the Poor.* London: Geoffrey Chapman, 1964.

Gheddo, Piero. *Why Is The Third World Poor?* Maryknoll: Orbis Books, 1973.

Gheerbrant, Alain. *The Rebel Church in Latin America.* Baltimore: Penguin Books, 1974.

Gibellini, Rosino (ed.). *Frontiers of Theology in Latin America.* London: SCM Press, 1980.

Gingerich, Melvin. *The Christian and Revolution.* Scottsdale, PA: Herald Press, 1968.

Gish, Arthur. *The New Left and Christian Radicalism.* Grand Rapids: Eerdmans, 1970.

Goldingay, John. "The hermeneutics of liberation theology," *Horizons in Biblical Theology: an International Dialogue* IV:1 (1982-1983), pp. 133-161.

————. "The Man of War and the Suffering Servant: The Old Testament and the Theology of Liberation," *Tyndale Bulletin* XXVII (1976), pp. 79-113.

Gollwitzer, Helmut. "Liberation in History," *Interpretation* XXVIII:4 (1974), pp. 404-421.

Gonzalez, Justo. *The Development of Christianity in the Latin Caribbean.* Grand Rapids: Eerdmans, 1969.

Gottwald, Norman K. *The Tribes of Yahweh: A Sociology of the Religion of Liberated Israel.* London: SCM Press, 1980, and Maryknoll: Orbis Books, 1979.

Grams, Monroe D. "Liberation Theology: Does It Really Liberate?" *Ministries* (Winter, 1984-85), pp. 92-93.

Grant, James P. and James W. Howe, "A critique from the United States," in Julio de Santa Ana (ed.), *To Break the Chains of Oppression,* Geneva: WCC, 1975, pp. 104-111.

Gremillion, Joseph (ed.). *The Gospel of Peace and Justice: Catholic Social Teaching since Pope John.* Maryknoll: Orbis Books, 1975.

Grenholm, Carl-Henric. *Christian Social Ethics in a Revolutionary Age.* Uppsala: Verbum, 1973.

Griffiths, Brian (ed.). *Is Revolution Change?* Downers Grove: Inter-Varsity Press, 1972.

Gruchy, John W. de. *Bonhoeffer and South Africa: theology in dialogue.* Grand Rapids: Eerdmans, 1984.

————. *Cry justice!: prayers, meditations and readings from South Africa.* Maryknoll: Orbis Books, 1986.

Guinness, Os. *Violence: A Study of Contemporary Attitudes.* Downers Grove: Inter-Varsity, 1974.

Gutierrez, Juan. *The New Libertarian Gospel: Pitfalls of the Theology of Liberation.* Chicago: Franciscan Herald Press, 1977.

Gutierrez, Gustavo. "Liberation Praxis and Christian Faith," in

Rosino Gibellini (ed.), *Frontiers of Theology in Latin America,* London: SCM Press, 1980, pp. 1-33.

Gutierrez, Gustavo. *The Power of the Poor in History.* Maryknoll: Orbis Books, 1983.

_____. *A Theology of Liberation: History, Politics and Salvation.* Maryknoll: Orbis Books, 1973.

_____. *We Drink from Our Own Wells: The Spiritual Journey of a People.* Maryknoll: Orbis Books, 1984.

Hall, Mary. *A Quest for the Liberated Christian.* Frankfurt: Lang, 1978.

Hanks, Thomas D. "How Ellul transcends liberation theologies," *TSF Bulletin* VIII:1 (1984), pp. 13-16.

_____. "Jacques Ellul: the original 'liberation theologian'," *TSF Bulletin* VII:5 (1984), pp. 8-11.

Hart, John William. *Topia and Utopia in Colombia and Peru,* unpublished doctoral dissertation for Union Theological Seminary of New York, 1978.

Hebblethwaite, Peter. "Christians and Instrumental Marxism," *The Month* VIII:11 (1975), pp. 312-317.

_____. "How Liberating Is Liberation Theology?," *Frontier* XVIII (1975), pp. 199-203.

Hengel, Martin. *Victory over Violence.* London: SPCK, 1975.

_____. *Was Jesus a Revolutionist?* Philadelphia: Fortress Press, 1971.

Hennelly, Alfred T. *Theologies in Conflict: The Challenge of Juan Luis Segundo.* New York: Orbis Books, 1979.

Henry, Carl F. H. "Insights on Liberation Theology," *United Evangelical Action* XLV:2 (1986), pp. 4-6.

_____. "The Modern Revolt against Authority," *God, Revelation and Authority,* Waco: Word Books, 1979, pp. 7-23.

_____ (ed.). *Revelation and the Bible.* Grand Rapids: Baker Book House, 1958.

Herrera, Altagracia Marina. *Man and the Latin American Church in the Theology of Liberation,* an unpublished doctoral dissertation for Fordham University, 1974.

Herzog, Frederick. "Introduction: on liberating liberation theology," in Hugo Assmann, *Theology for a Nomad Church,* Maryknoll: Orbis, 1976.

_____. "Liberation Theology as Ideology Critique?," *Interpretation* XXVIII:4 (1974), pp. 387-403.

_____. *Liberation Theology: Liberation in the Light of the Fourth Gospel.* New York: Seabury, 1972.

_____. "The Political Gospel," *Christian Century* LXXXVII:46 (1970), pp. 1380-1383.

_____. *Theology of the Liberating Word.* Nashville: Abingdon, 1971.

_____ and Gustavo Gutierrez. "Dealing with the true problems," *Books and Religion* XIII:2 (March, 1985), pp. 7-8.

Hodgson, Peter C. *New Birth of Freedom: A Theology of Bondage and Liberation.* Philadelphia: Fortress Press, 1976.

Holliday, Carolyn. *Liberation Theology in the Methodist Church of Brazil: Faith and Action in Six Methodist Education Institutions,* an unpublished doctoral dissertation for Saint Louis University, 1982.

Horner, Norman A. (ed.). *Protestant Crosscurrents in Mission.* Nashville: Abingdon, 1968.

Hornung, Warren G. *Paulo Freire's contribution to the theological education of the Protestant laity in Chile,* an unpublished doctoral dissertation for Claremont School of Theology, 1974.

House, H. Wayne. "An investigation of black liberation theology," *Bibliotheca Sacra* 139 (1982), pp. 159-176.

Houtart, Francois and Emile Pin. *The Church and the Latin American Revolution.* New York: Sheed and Ward, 1965.

Houtart, Francois and Andre Rousseau. *The Church and Revolution.* Maryknoll: Orbis Books, 1971.

Hromadka, Josef L. *Thoughts of a Czech Pastor.* London: SCM Press, 1970.

Hundley, Raymond C. "Book Review: *Liberation Theology* by J. Andrew Kirk," *Trinity Journal* (1982) pp. 233-237.

_____. "Book Review: *Exodus and Revolution* by Michael Walzer," *Eternity* XXXVI:11 (1985), p. 76.

_____. "How Long, O Lord?—A Sermon on the Gospel and Liberation," *Evangelical Review of Theology* X:2 (1986), pp. 164-173.

_____. "The Impact of Liberation Theology on Latin American Evangelicals," *United Evangelical Action* XLV:2 (1986), pp. 7-8.

_____. "Jesus, Habakkuk and Liberation Theology," *Outreach* 2 (1982), pp. 22-23.

_____. *Primer on Liberation Theology.* Greenwood, IN: OMSI, 1983.

_____. "Redemption and Deliverance/Liberation: A Biblical Model of Salvation Explored," a paper delivered to the Tyndale Fellowship Biblical Theology Study Group, Cambridge, England, July 4, 1980; on deposit at the Tyndale Library, Cambridge.

_____. "Storm over Latin America," *Outreach* 3 (1981), pp. 14-15; also published as "The Dangers of Liberation Theology," *Global Church Growth Bulletin* XVIII:6 (1981), pp. 149-150.

_____. *A Study of the Hermeneutical Theories and Methods of Selected Latin American Liberation Theologians,* an unpublished masters thesis for the University of Cambridge, 1982, on deposit in the University of Cambridge Library and the Asbury Theological Seminary Library.

Hunt, Chester. "Liberation theology in the Philippines: a test case," *Christianity Today* 26 (March 5, 1982), pp. 24-26.

Hutchinson, John (ed.). *Christian Faith and Social Action.* New York: Scribrners, 1953.

Hyun, Younghak. "Minjung theology and the religion of Han," *East Asian Journal of Theology* III:2 (1985), pp. 354-359.

Institute on Religion and Democracy. "The Church in Nicaragua: Decisive Test for Liberation Theology," Washington: IRD, September, 1984.

Kamaleson, Samuel T. "[Liberation Theology:] Fundamentally beneficial," *Together* 7 (1984), p. 15.

Kantzer, Kenneth S. "Unity and Diversity in Evangelical Faith," in David F. Wells (ed.), *The Evangelicals,* New York: Abingdon, 1975, pp. 39-52.

Kee, Alistair (ed.). *A Reader in Political Theology.* London: SCM Press, 1974.

———— (ed.). *Seeds of Liberation: Spiritual Dimension to Political Struggle.* London: SCM Press, 1973.

Keylock, Leslie R. "The Vatican tries to rein in a leading proponent of liberation theology," *Christianity Today* XXVIII:15 (1984), pp. 46-47.

Kinlaw, Dennis F. "Authority for the Church in Crisis," *Good News* (October/December, 1970), pp. 23-27.

Kirk, J. Andrew. "Beyond Capitalism and Marxism," *Theological Bulletin of the Latin American Theological Fraternity,* 1976.

————. "Edward Norman and political involvement," *Third Way* IV:1 (1980).

————. *Good news of the kingdom coming: the marriage of evangelism and social responsibility.* Leicester: Inter-Varsity, 1983.

————. "Is a Theology of Revolution Possible?," *Theological Fraternity Bulletin* 4 (February, 1973), pp. 1-14.

————. *Liberation Theology: An Evangelical View from the Third World.* Atlanta: Jon Knox, 1979.

————. "Liberation theology in Latin America today," *The Modern Churchman* XXIII:3 (1980), pp. 161-171.

————. "Marxism and the Church in Latin America," *Evangelical Review of Theology* III:1 (1979), pp. 107-118.

————. "The Meaning of Man in the debate between Christianity and Marxism," *Theological Fraternity Bulletin* 4 (February, 1973), pp. 1-14.

————. *Theology and the Third World church.* Leicester: Inter-Varsity, 1983.

————. *Theology Encounters Revolution.* Leicester: Inter-Varsity, 1980.

Kloppenburg, Bonaventure. *Temptations for the Theology of Liberation.* Chicago: Franciscan Herald Press, 1974.

Knapp, Stephen. "Critique—Miguez, Gutierrez: Pivotal Works," *Sojourners* V:7 (1976), pp. 33-37.

Kowalczyk, Stanislaw. "The Possibilities of Christian-Marxist Dialogue on Human Rights," *Soundings* LXVII:2 (1984), pp. 165-171.

Kretzchmar, Louise. *Black Theology in South Africa,* an unpublished masters thesis for the University of Cambridge, 1982.

Kuhn, Harold B. "Liberation Theology: A Semantic Approach," *The Wesley Theological Journal* XV:1 (Spring, 1980), pp. 34-45.

Kunst, Theo J. W. "The Kingdom of God and Social Justice," *Bibliotheca Sacra* CXL:558 (1983), pp. 108-116.

Lamb, Matthew. "Liberation Theology and Social Justice," *Process Studies* XIV:2 (1985), pp. 102-123.

Lane, Dermot. *Liberation Theology: An Irish Dialogue.* Dublin: Gill and Macmillan, 1977.

Lara-Braud, Jorge (ed.). *Our Claim on the Future.* New York: Friendship Press, 1970.

Lash, Nicholas. *A Matter of Hope: A Theologian's Reflections on the Thought of Karl Marx.* London: Darton, Longman and Todd, 1981.

The Latin American Theological Fraternity. "From Obedience to Proclamation: The Declaration of Jarabacoa," *Transformation* II:1 (1985), pp. 23-28.

Lausanne Committee for World Evangelization and the World Evangelical Fellowship. *Evangelism and Social Responsibility,* 1982.

Leech, Kenneth. "Liberation theology: the thought of Juan Luis Segundo," *Theology* 84 (1981), 258-266.

LeFevre, Perry D. "Liberation themes," *CTS Register* LXXV:1 (1985), pp. 1-41.

———. "Liberation theology: Latin America," *CTS Register* LXXII:2 (1982), pp. 22-29.

Leggett, Paul and John Stam. "Listening to Latin America—Communicating Across Cultures," *Christianity Today* (September 24, 1976), pp. 14-16.

Lehmann, Paul. *Ethics in a Christian Context.* New York: Harper and Row, 1963.

———. "A Theological Defense of Revolutions," *Worldview* (July-August, 1968), pp. 16-19.

———. *The Transfiguration of Politics: Jesus Christ and the Question of Revolution.* London: SCM Press, 1975.

Leiden, Carl and Karl M. Schmitt (eds.). *The Politics of Violence: revolution in the modern world.* Englewood Cliffs: Prentice-Hall, 1968.

Libanio, Joao Batista. "BECs in Socio-cultural Perspective," *Transformation* III:3 (1986), pp. 5-6.

Lopez Trujillo, Alfonso. *Liberation or Revolution?: An examination of the priest's role in the socio-economic class struggle in Latin America.* Huntington: Our Sunday Visitor, 1977.

Lowe, Kathy. "Liberation theology British style," *One World* 67 (1981), pp. 20-21.

MacEoin, Gary. "Liberation theology under fire," *Witness* LXVII:12 (1984), pp. 12-14.

Mackie, Steven G. "Liberation theology under attack," *International Review of Mission* 74 (1985), pp. 522-527.

Marquez, Robert. *Latin American Revolutionary Poetry/Poesia Revolucionaria Latinoamericana: A Bilingual Anthology.* New York/London: Monthly Review, 1974.

Mascall, E. L. *The Secularisation of Christianity: An Analysis and a Critique.* London: Darton, Longman and Todd, 1965.

Matheny, William E. "Keeping the main thing the main thing," *Fundamentalist Journal* II:9 (1983) pp. 50-52.

Maust, John. "Seminary Crisis a Case Study in Political, Doctrinal Tensions: Liberation theology is at issue in school's year of evaluation," *Christianity Today* (May 8, 1981), pp. 40-43.

Mbiti, John S. "Christianity and Traditional Religion in Africa," *International Review of Mission* 59 (1970), pp. 430-440.

————. *Concept of God in Africa.* London: SPCK, 1970.

McFadden, Thomas W. *Liberation, revolution and freedom.* New York: Seabury Press, 1975.

Meyer, Judith. "The roots of liberation theology," *Unitarian Universalist Christian* XL:3-4 (1985), pp. 9-16.

Migliore, Daniel L. "Jesus Christ, the reconciling liberator: the Confession of 1967 and theologies of liberation," *Journal of Presbyterian History* 62 (1983), pp. 33-42.

Miguez Bonino, Jose. "Christian Unity and Social Reconciliation: Consonance and Tension," *Study Encounter 36* IX:1 (1973), pp. 8ff.

————. "Christian Unity in Search of Locality," *Journal of Ecumenical Studies* VI (Spring, 1969), pp. 185-199.

————. *Christians and Marxists: The Mutual Challenge to Revolution.* Grand Rapids: Eerdmans, 1976, and London: Stodder and Stoughton, 1976.

————. "Christians and the Political Revolution," *Risk* III:1/2 (1967), pp. 100-110.

————. "The Church in a Turbulent Latin America," *This Month* 6 (March, 1974), pp. 3-5.

————. "Comments on 'Unity of the Church - Unity of Mankind'," *Ecumenical Review* 24 (1972), pp. 47-50.

————. "Common Witness and Proselytism, a Comment from Argentina," *Ecumenical Review* 23 (1971), pp. 35-37.

————. *Doing Theology in a Revolutionary Situation.* Philadelphia: Fortress Books, 1975 (also published as *Revolutionary Theology Comes of Age,* London: SPCK, 1975).

————(ed.). *Faces of Jesus: Latin American Christologies.* Maryknoll: Orbis Books, 1984.

————. "Five Theses Towards an Understanding of the 'Theology of Liberation'," *Expository Times* LXXXVII:7 (1976), pp. 196-200.

————. "Historical Praxis and Christian Identity," in Rosino Gibellini (ed.), *Frontiers of Theology in Latin America* pp. 260-283.

————. "How does United States presence in Latin America help, hinder or compromise mission in Latin America?", *Review and Expositor* LXXIV:2 (1977), pp. 173ff.

————. "Human and the System," *Theology Today* 35 (April, 1978), pp. 14-24.

————. "Is Fellowship Possible?", *Ecumenical Review* XXIV:4 (1972), pp. 459-470.

————. "A Latin American Attempt to Locate the Question of Unity," *Ecumenical Review* XXVI:2 (1974), pp. 210-221.

————. "Main Currents of Protestantism," in Samuel Shapiro (ed.), *Integration and Man and Society in Latin America,* Notre Dame: University of Notre Dame Press, 1967, pp. 191-201.

————. "Our Debt as Evangelicals to the Roman Catholic Community," *Ecumenical Review* XXI:4 (1969), pp. 310-319.

Miguez Bonino, Jose (ed.). *Out of the Hurt and Hope.* New York: Friendship Press, 1970.

———. "Poverty as Curse, Blessing and Challenge," *Iliff Review* 34 (1977), pp. 3-13.

———. "Roman Catholic Renewal in Latin America," *Frontier* V:3 (1962), p. 491.

———. *Room to Be People.* Philadelphia: Fortress Press, 1979.

———. "The Struggle of the Poor and the Church," *Ecumenical Review* XXVII:1 (1975), pp. 36-43.

———. *A Study of Some Recent Roman Catholic and Protestant Thought on the Relation of Scripture and Tradition,* unpublished doctoral dissertation for Union Theological Seminary of New York, 1960.

———. *Toward a Christian Political Ethic.* Philadelphia: Fortress Press, 1983.

———. "Violence: a theological reflection," *Ecumenical Review* 25 (1973), pp. 68-74 (also published as "Violence and Liberation," *Christianity and Crisis* 32, 1972, pp. 169-172).

———. "Whose Human Righs? A historic-theological meditation," *International Review of Mission* LXVI:262 (1977), pp. 220-224.

Minella, Mary J. "Praxis and the question of revelation," *Iliff Review* 36 (1979), pp. 17-29.

Miranda, Jose Porfirio. *Being and the Messiah: The Message of St. John.* Maryknoll: Orbis Books, 1977.

———. *Communism in the Bible.* Maryknoll: Orbis Books, 1982.

———. *Marx Against the Marxists: The Christian Humanism of Karl Marx.* London: SCM Press, 1980, and Maryknoll: Orbis Books, 1980.

———. *Marx and the Bible.* London: SCM Press, 1977, and Maryknoll: Orbis Books, 1977.

Moellering, Ralph L. "The crisis in Latin America and liberation theology," *Academy* XXXVIII:3-4 (1982), pp. 168-192.

Moltmann, Jurgen. *The Gospel of Liberation.* Waco: Word, 1973.

———. "An Open Letter to Jose Miguez Bonino: on Latin American liberation theology," *Christianity and Crisis* (March 26, 1976), pp. 57-63.

———. *Religion, revolution and the future.* New York: Charles Scribner's Sons 1969.

Morrison, Roy D. "Process philosophy, social thought and liberation theology," *Zygon* 19 (1984), pp. 65-81.

Nash, Ronald H. *Freedom, Justice and the State.* Lanham, MD: University Press of America, 1980.

——— (ed.). *Liberation Theology.* Milford, MI: Mott Media, 1984.

———. *The New Evangelicalism.* Grand Rapids: Zondervan, 1963.

National Conference of Catholic Bishops. *Puebla: Evangelization at Present and in the Future of Latin America—Conclusions.* London: Catholic Institute for International Relations, 1980.

Neely, Anan Preston. *Protestant Antecedents of the Latin American Theology of Liberation,* an unpublished doctoral dissertation for the American University, Washington, 1977.

Norman, Edward. *Christianity and the World Order.* Oxford/New York: Oxford University Press, 1979.

Novak, Michael (ed.). *Capitalism and Socialism: A Theological Inquiry.* Washington: American Enterprise Institute for Public Policy Research, 1979.

————. *The Corporation: a theological inquiry.* Washington: American Enterprise Institute for Public Policy Research, 1981.

————. "Democratic Capitalism: A North American Liberation Theology," *Transformation* II:1 (1985), pp. 18-23.

————. *Denigration of Capitalism.* Washington: American Enterprise Institute for Public Policy Research, 1979.

————. *Freedom with Justice: Catholic Social Thought and Liberal Institutions.* New York: Harper and Row, 1984.

————. *Liberation South, Liberation North.* Washington: American Enterprise Institute for Public Policy Research, 1981.

————. *Speaking to the Third World: essays on democracy and development.* Washington: American Enterprise Institute for Public Policy Research, 1985.

————. *The Spirit of Democratic Capitalism.* Greenville, NC: S & S Publications, 1982.

————. *A Theology for Radical Politics.* New York: Herder and Herder, 1969.

————. "Why Latin America Is Poor," *The Atlantic Monthly,* March, 1982, pp. 69-75.

————. *Will It Liberate?: Questions about Liberation Theology.* Mahwah, NJ: Paulist Press, 1986.

Novak, Michael and Michael P. Jackson. *Latin America: Dependency or Interdependence?* Washington: American Enterprise Institute for Public Policy Research, 1985.

Nunez C., Emilio A. *Liberation Theology.* Chicago: Moody Press, 1985.

————. "The Theology of Liberation in Latin America," *Evangelical Review of Theology* III:1 (1979), pp. 37-49.

O'Connor, James Thomas. *Liberation: towards a theology for the Church in the world, according to the second General Conference of Latin American Bishops at Medellin, 1968.* Rome: Officium Libri Catholici, 1972.

O'Donnell, James G. "The influence of Freud's hermeneutic of suspicion on the writings of Juan Segundo," *Journal of Psychology and Theology* 10 (1982), pp. 28-34.

Ogden, Schubert M. *Faith and Freedom: toward a theology of liberation.* Nashville: Abingdon, 1979, and Belfast: Christian Journals, 1979.

Okolo, Chukwudum B. "Liberation theology and the African church," *Bulletin de theologie africaine* IV:8 (1982), pp. 173-187.

Opocensky, Milan. *Christians and Revolutions: A breakthrough in Christian thought.* Geneva: WSCF, 1977.

Orme, John. "Reflections on the Political-Apocalyptic Concept of Liberation according to St. Paul," *Theological Fraternity Bulletin* 3 (1974), pp. 12-16.

Osborn, Robert T. "Some problems of liberation theology," *Journal of the American Academy of Religion* 51 (1983), pp. 79-95.

Osborne, Grant. "Theologians from North, South, and Central America gather in Mexico," *Christianity Today* XXVIII:1 (January 13, 1984), pp. 60 and 64.

Padilla, C. Rene. "Evangelism and Social Responsibility from Wheaton '66 to Wheaton '83," *Transformation* II:3 (1985), pp. 27-33.

————. "God's Word and Man's Myths," *Theological Fraternity Bulletin* 2 (1977), pp. 1-12.

————. "The Interpreted Word: Reflections on Contextual Hermeneutics," *Themelios* VII:1 (1981), pp. 18-23.

————. *Mission between the Times: essays on the kingdom.* Grand Rapids: Eerdmans, 1985.

————. *The New Face of Evangelicalism: A Symposium on the Lausanne Covenant.* London: Hodder and Stoughton, 1976.

————. "The Theology of Liberation," *Christianity Today* XVIII:3 (November 9, 1973), p. 69.

Pantelis M., Jorge. *Kingdom of God and Church in the Historical Process of Liberation: Latin American Perspective,* an unpublished doctoral dissertation for Union Theological Seminary of New York, 1977.

Paz, Nestor. *My life for my friends: The guerrilla journal of Nestor Paz.* New York: Orbis Books, 1975.

Periera, Oscar. "Salvation in the Prophets," *Theological Fraternity Bulletin* 3 (1975), pp. 26-33.

Perez, Pablo. "Liberationistic Roots in Latin America," *Theological Fraternity Bulletin* 3 (1974), pp. 9-12.

Perez-Esclarin, Antonio. *Atheism and Liberation.* London: SCM Press, 1980.

Peruvian Bishops' Commission for Social Action. *Between Honesty and Hope.* Maryknoll: Orbis Books, 1970.

Petulla, Joseph M. *Christian Political Theology: A Marxian Guide.* Maryknoll: Orbis Books, 1972.

Phillips, Steven. *The Use of Scripture in Liberation Theologies,* an unpublished doctoral dissertation for Southern Baptist Theological Seminary, 1978.

Pinnock, Clark. "An Evangelical Theology of Human Liberation," *Sojourners* 5 (February, 1976), pp. 30-33, and (March, 1976), pp. 26-29.

————. "Liberation Theology: The Gains, the Gaps," *Christianity Today* XV (1976), pp. 13-15.

Pixley, George. "The Poor Evangelize Biblical Scholarship," *American Baptist Quarterly* II:2 (1983), pp. 157-167.

Plowman, Edward E. "The Archbishop Calls for the Gospel, Not Marxism, in Nicaragua," *Christianity Today* XXVI:3 (1982), pp. 72.

Quigley, Thomas E. (ed.). *Freedom and unfreedom in the Americas: Towards a theology of liberation.* New York: IDOC, 1971.

Ramm, Bernard. *The Evangelical Heritage.* Waco: Word Books,

1973.

Ramm, Bernard. *Special Revelation and the Word of God.* Grand Rapids: Eerdmans, 1961.

Ranly, Ernest W. "The liberating gospel according to Alfredo Fierro," *Encounter* 42 (1981), pp. 189-196.

Richard, Pablo (ed.). *The Idols of Death and the God of Life: A Theology.* Maryknoll: Orbis books, 1983.

Ricoeur, Paul. *The Conflict of Interpretations.* Evanston: Northwestern University Press, 1975.

————. *History and Truth.* Evanston: Northwestern University Press, 1965.

Robb, Carol Sue. *Integration of Marxist Constructs into the Theology of Liberation from Latin America,* an unpublished doctoral dissertation for Boston University Graduate School, 1978.

Roberts, J. Deotis. "Liberation theologies: a critical essay," *The Journal of the Interdenominational Theological Center* 9 (1981), pp. 85-89.

Roberts, W. Dayton, "Venezuelan Agenda," *Together* 7 (a publication of World Vision, 1985), pp. 6-10.

————. "Where Has Liberation Theology Gone Wrong?," *Christianity Today* (October 19, 1979), pp. 27-30.

Romero, Archbishop Oscar Arnulfo. *The Church, political organization and violence.* London: Catholic Institute for International Relations, 1980.

Romero, Claude Gilbert. *A Hermeneutic of Appropriation: A Case Study of Method in the Prophet Jeremiah and Latin American Liberation Theology,* an unpublished doctoral dissertation for Princeton Theological Seminary, 1982.

Ruether, Rosemary Radford. "The bible and the religious left: an interview with Rosemary Radford Ruether," *Witness* LXVI:3 (1983), pp. 8-9 and 17-18.

————. *Liberation Theology.* New York: Paulist Press, 1972.

————. *The Radical Kingdom: The Western Experience of Messianic Hope.* New York: Harper and Row, 1970.

————. *Womanguides: Readings towards a Feminist Theology.* Boston: Beacon Press, 1986.

Russel, Letty M. *Human Liberation in a Feminist Perspective—A Theology.* Philadelphia: Westminster Press, 1974.

Russell, George. "Taming the Liberation Theologians," *Time* (February 4, 1985), pp. 56-59.

Rutschman, LaVerne A. "Anabaptism and liberation theology," *The Mennonite Quarterly Review* 55 (1981), pp. 255-270.

————. "Latin American liberation theology and radical Anabaptism," *Journal of Ecumenical Studies* 19 (1982), pp. 38-56.

Santa Ana, Julio de. "Christian presence in a revolutionary society," in G. Hoffman and W. Wille (eds.). *World Mission and World Communism,* Edinburgh: The Saint Andrew Press, 1970.

————. "Domination and Dependence," *One World* 5 (April, 1975), pp. 20-21.

————. *Good News to the Poor: The Challenge of the Poor in the*

History of the Church. Geneva: WCC, 1977.

Santa Ana, Julio de. "The Influence of Bonhoeffer on the Theology of Liberation," *Ecumenical Review* XXVIII:2 (1976), pp. 188-197.

————. "The Latin American Masses: The Unsatisfied Ones," *Student World* (1964), pp. 21-30.

————. "The Migration Debate at the W.C.C. Nairobi Assembly," *Migration Today* 20 (1976), pp. 97-101.

————. "Revelation and the Meaning of History," *Student World* 60 (1967), pp. 325-337.

———— (ed.). *Separation without Hope?* Geneva: WCC, 1978.

———— (ed.). *To Break the Chains of Oppression*. Geneva: WCC, 1976.

———— (ed.). *Towards a Church of the Poor*. Geneva: WCC, 1979.

————. "What the Ecumenical Movement Expects from Puebla," in IDOC, *The Church at the Crossroads,* Rome: IDOC International, 1978; pp. 148ff.

Savolainen, James William. *Theology in the Shadow of Marx,* an unpublished doctoral dissertation for the Lutheran School of Theology at Chicago, 1982.

Schaeffer, Francis A. *The Great Evangelical Disaster*. Westchester, IL: Crossway Books, 1984.

————. *How Shall We Then Live?* Old Tappan, NJ: Fleming H. Revell, 1976.

Schall, James V. *Liberation Theology in Latin America*. San Francisco: Ignatius Press, 1982.

Schipani, Daniel S. "Conscientization and creativity: a reinterpretation of Paulo Freire," *Religious Education* 78 (1983), pp. 418-419.

Schubeck, Thomas Louis. *Liberation and Imagination,* an unpublished doctoral dissertation for the University of Southern California, 1975.

Segundo, Juan Luis. *Faith and Ideologies*. Maryknoll: Orbis Books, 1985.

————. *The Historical Jesus of the Synoptics*. Maryknoll: Orbis Books, 1985.

————. *The Liberation of Theology*. Maryknoll: Orbis Books, 1976.

————. "Possible Contribution of Protestant Theology to Latin American Christianity in the Future," *Lutheran Quarterly* 22 (February, 1970), pp. 60-68.

————. "The shift within Latin American theology," *Journal of Theology for Southern Africa* 52 (1985), pp. 17-29.

————. *Theology and the Church: A Response to Cardinal Ratzinger and a Warning to the Whole Church*. Minneapolis: Winston Press, 1985.

————. *A Theology for Artisans of a New Humanity,* five volumes. Maryknoll: Orbis Books, 1973-1974.

Semmel, Bernard, *The Methodist Revolution*. New York: Basic Books, 1973.

Shaull, Richard. "The Church and Revolutionary Change: Contrasting Perspectives," in Henry A. Landsberger (ed.), *The Church and Social Change in Latin America,* Notre Dame: University of

Notre Dame Press, 1970.

Shaull, Richard. "Does Religion Demand Social Change?," *Theology Today* XXVI (1969/1970), pp. 5-13.

_____. *Encounter with Revolution.* New York: Association Press, 1955.

_____. "The End of the Road and New Beginning," in John C. Raines and Thomas Dean (eds.), *Marxism and Radical Religion,* Philadelphia: Temple University Press, 1970.

_____. "From Somewhere Along the Road," *Theology Today* XXIX:1 (1972), pp. 86-101.

_____. "From the pulpit: the call of Moses," *Church and Society* LXV:4 (1985), pp. 25-31.

_____. "The Revolutionary Challenge to Church and Theology," *Theology Today* XXIII:4 (1967), pp. 470-480.

_____. "The Second Latin American Church and Society Conference," *Christian Century* XXVI:7 (1966/1967), pp. 89-91.

_____. "A Theological Perspective on Human Liberation," in IDOC (ed.), *When All Else Fails: Christian Arguments on Violent Revolution,* Philadelphia: Pilgrim Press, 1970.

_____. "Theology and the Transformation of Society," *Theology Today* XXV:1 (1968), pp. 23-36.

Shaull, Richard and Gustavo Gutierrez. *Liberation and Change.* Atlanta: John Knox Press, 1977.

Shejaval, Abisai. *The Idea of God in Liberation Theology,* an unpublished doctoral dissertation for the Aquinas Institute of Theology, 1978.

Sider, Ronald. "An Evangelical Vision for Public Policy," *Transformation* II:3 (1985), pp. 1-9.

_____. *Evangelicals and Development: Towards a Theology of Social Change.* Exeter: Paternoster Press, 1981.

_____ (ed.). *Evangelism, Salvation and Social Justice.* Bramcote, Nottingham: Grove Books, 1977.

_____. *Rich Christians in an Age of Hunger.* London: Hodder and Stoughton, 1979.

Simmons, Paul D. "Capitalism: A Theological Critique," *Review and Expositor* LXXXI:2 (1984), pp. 181-195.

Sinclair, John H. (ed.). *Protestantism in Latin America: A Bibliographic Guide.* South Pasadena, CA: William Carey Library, 1976.

Slade, Stan. "Liberation Anthropology: Segundo's Use of Teilhard de Chardin," *Studia Biblica et Theologica* IX:1 (April, 1979).

Smith, Simon E. "The Vatican document on liberation theology," *African Ecclesial Review* 26 (1984), pp. 372-373.

Smith, Timothy L. *Revivalism and Social Reform.* New York: Harper and Row, 1956.

Snoek, C. J. "The Third World, Revolution and Christianity," *Concilium* V:2 (1966).

Snyder, Howard A. *The Radical Wesley.* Downers Grove: Inter-Varsity, 1980.

Sobrino, Jon. *Christology at the Crossroads.* Maryknoll: Orbis

Books, 1978.

Stam, John. "Christian witness in Central America: a radical evangelical perspective," *Transformation* II:1 (1985), pp. 14-17.

Stott, John R. W. *The Lausanne Covenant.* Minneapolis: World Wide, 1975.

————. "Seeking Theological Agreement: The Consultation on the Relationship between Evangelism and Social Responsibility," *Transformation* I:1 (1984), pp. 21-22.

Strain, Charles R. "Liberation theology: North American perspectives," *Religious Studies Review* 8 (1982), pp. 239-244.

Stringfellow, William. "The Bible and Ideology," *Sojourners* V:7 (1976), pp. 6-7.

Stumme, John R. *Socialism in Theological Perspective: A Study of Paul Tillich 1918-1933.* Missoula, Montana: Scholars Press, 1978.

Sturm, Douglas. "Ratzinger's 'J'accuse'," *Christianity and Crisis* 44 (1984), pp. 437-439.

Tambasco, Anthony J. *The Bible for Ethics: Juan Luis Segundo and First World Ethics.* Lanham, MD: University Press of America, 1980.

————. "Contribution of J. L. Segundo to the question of the hermeneutical relationship of the Bible to Christian ethics," *Religious Education* 78 (1983), p. 425.

————. "Pauline Ethics: An Application of Liberation Hermeneutics," *Biblical Theology Bulletin* XII:4 (1982), pp. 125-127.

Taylor, Bron. "Authority in ethics: a portrait of the methodology of Sojourners Fellowship," *Encounter* 46 (1985), pp. 139-156.

Thomas, M. M. *The Christian Response to the Asian Revolution.* London: SCM Press, 1968.

————. *Salvation and Humanisation.* Bangalore: CISRS, 1971.

Thomas, Norman E. "Evangelism and liberation theology," *Missiology* 9 (1981), pp. 473-484.

Thrower, James. "Marxism: the liberation of theology or a theology of liberation?", *Theology* 87 (1984), pp. 420-426.

Ton, Josif. *The Christian Manifesto: The Place of the Christian in the Socialist Society.* Keston: Keston College, 1976.

Topel, L. John. *The Way to Peace: Liberation through the Bible.* Maryknoll: Orbis Books, 1979.

Torres, Camilo. *Revolutionary Writings.* New York: Harper and Row, 1972.

Torres, Sergio and John Eagleson (eds.). *The Challenge of Basic Christian Communities.* Maryknoll: Orbis Books, 1981.

————. *Theology in the Americas.* Maryknoll: Orbis Books, 1976.

Torres, Sergio and Virginia Fabella (eds.). *The Emergent Gospel: theologies from the underside of history.* Maryknoll: Orbis Books, 1978.

Torres, Ulises. "The theological judgment from Latin America," *Engage/Social Action* 11 (1983), pp. 39-43.

Tutu, Desmond. *Crying in the Wilderness.* Grand Rapids: Eerdmans, 1982.

————. "God - black or white?," *Ministry* XI:4 (1971), pp. 111-115.

Tutu, Desmond. "God-given Dignity and the Quest for Liberation in the Light of the South African Dilemma," in D. Thomas (ed.), *Liberation*, SACC Papers, 1976, pp. 53-59.

————. *Hope and Suffering: sermons and speeches*. Grand Rapids: Eerdmans, 1984.

————. "The Theology of Liberation in Africa," in K. Appiah-Kubi and Sergio Torres (eds.), *African Theology en Route*, pp. 162-168.

Vanderhoff, Frank Paul. *Bibliography: Latin American Theology of Liberation*. Cuernavaca: Centro Intercultural de Documentacion, 1972.

Vekemans, Roger. *Bibliography: Church and Liberation, Development and Liberation*. Cuernavaca: Centro Intercultural de Documentacion, 1973.

Verkuyl, Johannes. *Responsible revolution*. Grand Rapids: Eerdmans, 1974.

Wagner, C. Peter (ed.). *A Catalog of the C. Peter Wagner Collection of Materials on Latin American Theology of Liberation*. Pasadena: Fuller Theological Seminary, 1974.

————. *Latin American Theology: Radical or Evangelical?* Grand Rapids: Eerdmans, 1970.

Wallis, Jim. *Agenda for Biblical People*. New York: Harper and Row, 1984.

————. "Liberation and Conformity," *Sojourners* V:7 (1976), pp. 3-4.

Wang, Joseph. "Latin American Liberation Theology," *The Asbury Seminarian* XXXII:3 (1977), pp. 18-39.

Weir, J. Emmette. "The Bible and Marx: a discussion of the hermeneutics of liberation theology," *Scottish Journal of Theology* XXXV:4 (1982), pp. 337-350.

————. "Liberation theology—Marxist or Christian?," *Expository Times* 90 (1979), pp. 260-261.

Wells, David F. *The Search for Salvation*. Leicester: Inter-Varsity, 1978.

Westhelle, Vitor. "Dependency theory: some implications for liberation theology," *Dialog* 20 (1981), pp. 293-299.

White, Leland J. "Biblical theologians and theologies of liberation" (two parts), *Biblical Theology Bulletin* 11 (April, 1981), pp. 35-40, and 11 (October, 1981), pp. 98-103.

Wigglesworth, Chris. "Evangelical Views of the Poor and Social Ethics Today," *Tyndale Bulletin* 35 (1984), pp. 162-184.

————. "Which Way to Utopia: with Marx or Jesus?," *Evangelical Review of Theology* I (1977/78), pp. 95-107.

Williamson, Rene de Visme. "The Theology of Liberation," *Christianity Today* 19 (August 8, 1975), pp. 7-13.

Willmer, Hadden (ed.). *Christian Faith and Political Hopes: A Reply to E. R. Norman*. London: Epworth, 1977.

Wilmore, Gayraud S. *Black Religion and Black Radicalism*. New York: Doubleday and Anchor Press, 1972.

————. "The Path toward Racial Justice," *Journal of Presbyterian History* LXI:1 (1983), pp. 110-117.

Wilmore, Gayraud S. and James H. Cone. *Black Theology: A Docu-*

mentary History, 1966 - 1979. New York: Orbis Books, 1979.

Winter, Derek. *Hope in Captivity: The Prophetic Church in Latin America.* London: Epworth Press, 1977.

World Council of Churches, "Declaration of Golconda," Latin American Department, July 24-26, 1969; Geneva, Switzerland.

Yoder, John H. *Christian Witness to the State.* Newton, KS: Faith and Life Press, 1977.

———. *The Original Revolution.* Scottsdale, PA: Herald Press, 1971.

———. *The Politics of Jesus.* Grand Rapids: Eerdmans, 1972.

———. *The Priestly Kingdom: Social Ethics as Gospel.* Notre Dame: University of Notre Dame Press, 1986.

———. "Probing the Meaning of Liberation," *Sojourners* V:7 (1976), pp. 27-29.

———. *What Would You Do?* Scottsdale, PA: Herald Press, 1983.

———. *When War Is Unjust: Being Honest in Just-War Thinking.* Minneapolis: Augsburg, 1984.

Zorrilla, Hugo. "Liberty in Pauline Thought," *Theological Fraternity Bulletin* 2 (1975), pp. 1-23.

Bibliographic Essay

The study of Liberation Theology is a complex under-taking, not only because there are so many kinds of liberation theologies, but also because it represents a new area of research whose definitions and delimita-tions are still in a fairly fluid form. The present work has been an attempt to establish some of those definitions and to describe the limits of this theological movement in terms of its characteristics and antecedents. There is a need for a great deal more research on Liberation Theology: the relationship between ideology and theol-ogy; its philosophical foundations; its hermeneutical dependency on European hermeneutes such as Gada-mer, Ricoeur, Schleiermacher and others; its theological antecedents; its historical development; critiques of it; and related subjects, such as justice, oppression, the kingdom of God, the base community churches, vio-lence, politics, revolution, humanization, poverty/ wealth, eschatology and social action, the social minis-try of the Church, exegetical theology and many more. The purpose of this bibliographic essay is to encourage and facilitate that research, noting basic works for those with a casual interest in the subject and in-depth information for those who want to pursue this fascinat-ing subject more fully. All of the works cited in this essay appear in this book's English language bibliog-raphy.

I. *General Introduction:*

For those wishing to read general, introductory mate-rials on Liberation Theology, *Liberation Theology* by Emilio Nunez is a very helpful companion to this book. Nunez is a highly respected Latin American evangelical leader who has been active in the most important events in the development of Liberation Theology, especially among Protestants. His book is well-organized and fair in its evaluations and criticisms. Andrew Kirk's *Liberation Theology* is also helpful, although its organization does not make it quite as clear as Nunez' book. Kirk does offer extensive quotes from liberation theologians which will be difficult to unravel for those not deeply immersed in theological jargon. Still, he offers the reader a good opportunity to hear the liberationists speak for themselves.

Those looking for a brief, to-the-point presentation of Liberation Theology's basic elements can read several short articles. My "Storm over Latin America" and "Book Review: *Liberation Theology* by J. Andrew Kirk" give just such a basic presentation. Nunez has also published a very good article, "The Theology of Liberation in Latin America," which is especially helpful in tracing the development of this theology. Rene Padilla has written a good introductory article entitled, "The Theology of Liberation." Liberationist Jose Miguez Bonino wrote a brief article in 1976 ("Five Theses Towards an Understanding of the 'Theology of Liberation'") in which he attempted to communicate the five foundational assumptions of Liberation Theology in a way that Western theologians could understand. His article offers a good introduction to the basic content of Liberation Theology from one of its proponents. For an early theological presentation of Liberation Theology, see Rubem Alves' "Theses for a Reconstruction of Theology" (1970).

II. *History of the Development of Liberation Theology:*

Several profitable books have been written which give a brief history of the development of Liberation Theology. Nunez' *Liberation Theology* gives an excellent historical synopsis (pp. 17-127). Kirk's *Liberation Theology* does the same, placing greater emphasis on its development among Roman Catholics (pp. 3-28). However some of his early Latin American historical sections may be a bit exaggerated in some details. The best sources for the Protestant historical background of Liberation Theology are Alan Neely's doctoral dissertation, *Protestant Antecedents of the Latin American Theology of Liberation,* and Orlando Costas' *Theology of the Crossroads in Contemporary Latin America.* Enrique Dussel offers an insightful, if somewhat prejudiced, reading of the historical development of Liberation Theology among Latin American Roman Catholics in his book, *History and the Theology of Liberation,* pp. 75-138. I am currently writing a work detailing the history of the development of this theology from 1950 to 1986.

Those interested in reading shorter articles dealing with the history of Liberation Theology in a more personal, autobiographical way will find Richard Shaull's "From Somewhere Along the Road" and Rubem Alves' "Confessions: On Theology and Life" very instructive. Also, Julio de Santa Ana's article revealing the strategic role of the writings of Dietrich Bonhoeffer in the early Protestant antecedents to Liberation Theology gives a tantalizing glimpse of some of the thoughts which gave birth to this theology ("The Influence of Bonhoeffer on the Theology of Liberation").

III. *Precursors of Liberation Theology:*

Ernst Bammel (who was my tutor at Cambridge) has done an excellent job of tracing the major revolutionary interpretations of Christianity from Reimarus (1777) to Brandon (1967) in his chapter, "The revolutionary theory from Reimarus to Brandon." He also includes some interesting commentary on Liberation Theology in his discussion.

There is a great need for further study on the background of the ideas that finally surfaced in Liberation Theology. One interesting study would be the investigation of four Latin American Roman Catholics whose thoughts paved the way for the elaboration of Liberation Theology in that church: Paulo Freire, Dom Helder Camara, Camilo Torres and Ernesto Cardenal. Dussel discusses the social context of their influence in *History and the Theology of Liberation,* pp. 116-138.

Paulo Freire worked out a plan to teach people to read and, at the same time, show them the oppressive state they live in and what to do about it by supporting others to change history. This process, termed "conscientizacion" in Spanish, became a watchword of Liberation Theology and is spelled out by Freire in his book, *Pedagogy of the Oppressed.*

Dom Helder Camara proposed the idea of a "spiral of violence" in Latin America in which injustice produces revolt which produces repression and further injustice. The process continues with increasing violence, suffering and bloodshed. Camara proposed non-violent protest to break this spiral, but the liberationists rejected that part of his argument and insisted on violent revolution as the only solution. Still, Camara's *Spiral of Violence* has had great influence throughout Latin America and is worthy of careful study. Jose de Broucker has written two books on Camara based on extensive interviews with the Archbishop. They make excellent reading for those who wish to understand the thinking of a Latin American moderate who is as strongly against "capitalist imperialism" as the liberationists but who has chosen the way of peace, not violence, to destroy it. Also, see Mary Hall's depiction of Camara in *A Quest for the Liberated Christian.*

Camilo Torres was the "revolutionary priest" from Colombia who felt he had to join the Marxist revolution to express Christian love effectively. Killed by Colombian troops in a battle, Torres has become "a universal symbol" of sacrificial Christian love expressed through violent revolution according to Dussel. Torres' works, *Revolutionary Writings,* are thought-provoking and challenging.

Ernesto Cardenal, who is now a member of the Sandinista ruling cabinet in Nicaragua, founded a community on the archipelago in Lake Nicaragua called Solentiname. There he taught the campesinos that they could read and interpret the Bible better than any theologians, and he began "gospel dialogues" in which the members of the community voiced their revolutionary interpretations of selected biblical passages. Some of these dialogues have been preserved in Cardenal's *Love in Practice* and are quite astonishing.

Five important theologians from Europe and North America—Bloch, Gauthier, Ricoeur, Bonhoeffer, Hromadka and Lehmann—had great influence on the development of Liberation Theology, especially in the beginning stages. Tracing their influences on Liberation Theology must begin with a look at their most pertinent works.

Ernst Bloch's views on the god-destroying, revolutionary character of authentic Christianity can be seen in his *Atheism in Christianity*.

Father Paul Gauthier's influence was felt during Vatican II when he met with the bishops of Latin America and spoke to them about the need to become the "Church of the poor" which he explained in his book, *Christ, the Church and the Poor*.

Paul Ricoeur's hermeneutical emphases on seeing Scripture as a collection of "symbols" with a "reserve of meaning" greatly influenced liberationist hermeneute, Jose Severino Croatto. Ricoeur's hermeneutical theories can be seen in his works, *The Conflict of Interpretations* and *History and Truth*.

The concepts used by the liberationists from Dietrich Bonhoeffer center around his book, *Letters and Papers from Prison*. In it they found justification for the use of violence for revolutionary action against tyranny.

Josef Hromadka wrote articles for the early ISAL publications in which he urged the ISAL leaders to follow Marxist socialism as the best vehicle for establishing a just society and argued that atheism is not an essential part of Marxism. Hromadka's *Thoughts of a Czech Pastor* detail these perspectives.

Finally, we have seen Paul Lehmann's decisive influence on Protestant liberationists. His thoughts on politics, revolution and Marxism can be studied in *Ethics in a Christian Context, The Transfiguration of Politics* and "A Theological Defense of Revolutions." The study of these "precursors of Liberation Theology" should lead, after a thorough examination of their own works, to a careful study of the way their thoughts surface in the writings of the liberation theologians.

IV. *Representative Liberation Theologians:*

Those who would like to read a well-selected compilation of short essays from prominent liberation theologians such as Gutierrez, Boff, Assmann, Segundo, Miguez Bonino and Alves should see Rosino Gibellini's *Frontiers of Theology in Latin America*. If you are interested in reading the clearest presentations of Liberation Theology, I would suggest beginning with Gustavo Gutierrez' *A Theology of Liberation* and Jose Miguez Bonino's two works, *Doing Theology in a Revolutionary Situation* and *Christians and Marxists*. Those three books offer the best-organized and most coherent explanation of Liberation Theology by liberationists in English. To supplement these with a liberationist work which is a bit more radical and militant than those of Gutierrez and Miguez Bonino, read Hugo Assmann's *Theology for a Nomad Church*.

After perusing those presentations of Liberation Theology, those who want to research at greater depth should read the books and articles by each of the following liberation theologians (in chronological order, if possible, to see the evolution of each individual theologian's thought): Rubem Alves, Leonardo Boff, Jose Severino Croatto, Gustavo Gutierrez, Jose Miguez Bonino, Jose Porfirio Miranda and Juan Luis Segundo. Liberationists of secondary importance are: Ernesto Cardenal, Joseph Comblin, Enrique Dussel, Orlando Fals-Borda, Paulo Freire, Segundo Galilea, Ivan Illich, Nestor Paz, Antonio Perez-Esclarin, Julio de Santa Ana, Richard Shaull, Jon Sobrino, John Stam, Camilo Torres, Sergio Torres and Raul Vidales.

V. *Analysis of the Exegesis and Hermeneutics of Liberation Theology:*

The foundational consideration in the analysis of

Liberation Theology is its exegetical and hermeneutical theory and method. There are several in-depth studies which would enlighten any serious study of this theology. Howard Dahl has written a master's thesis, *Praxis: A Ground for Truth?*, for Trinity Evangelical Divinity School. In it he explores the problems inherent in making "praxis" the starting point of theology. Dahl rightly considers this to be the primary weakness in Liberation Theology. My thesis for the University of Cambridge, *A Study of the Hermeneutical Theories and Methods of Selected Latin American Liberation Theologians,* deals directly with these exegetical and hermeneutical considerations as well. Steven Phillips has written a doctoral dissertation, *The Use of Scripture in Liberation Theologies,* which also focuses on these issues. Finally, Claude Romero has explored the points of comparison and contrast between the hermeneutics of the prophet Jeremiah and those of Latin American liberationists in his dissertation, *A Hermeneutic of Appropriation.*

Among the liberationists themselves, the theologian who has done the most writing on hermeneutics is Jose Severino Croatto. Unfortunately not many of his works have been translated into English, but his book, *Exodus: a hermeneutic of freedom,* will give readers a fair idea of his hermeneutical theories. Jose Miguez Bonino devoted a chapter of his book, *Doing Theology in a Revolutionary Situation,* to the subject of hermeneutics (pp. 86-105). In it he clarifies his rejection of the traditional theological approach of "applying biblical truth to life" and his advocacy of "praxis" as the starting point of Liberation Theology. I hope to publish a major work on the exegetical theology of the radical liberationists in the near future.

VI. *Favorable Analysis of Liberation Theology:*

It is always enlightening to read the analysis of "outsiders," who substantially agree with the liberationists. Robert McAfee Brown of the United States has publicly voiced his support of this theology and has even refused to speak his native language in a World Council of

Churches Assembly because he saw it as "linguistic imperialism." His book, *Theology in a New Key,* and article, "Drinking from our own wells," give a very sympathetic view of Liberation Theology from a North American theologian's perspective.

J. G. Davies of the University of Birmingham offers a favorable perspective on Liberation Theology in pages 100-187 of his book, *Christians, Politics and Violent Revolution,* where he deals with the question of when Christians may participate in violent revolutions.

John Stam, once a professor at the Latin American Mission Seminary in San Jose, Costa Rica, now teaches in Nicaragua. Although he was born in the United States, he has become one of the strongest liberationist voices in Latin America. The article he co-authored with Paul Leggett, "Listening to Latin America," is a mild version of his views, while "Christian witness in Central America: a radical evangelical perspective" comes much closer to the reality of his position.

In his book, *Hope in Captivity,* Derek Winter takes us on a tour of Latin America in which he chats with several leaders of the liberationist movement and observes the realities of Latin American life.

Perhaps a surprise entry in this list of those favorable to Liberation Theology will be the name of Dr. Samuel Kamaleson, who once served as the vice president of World Vision. In his article, "Fundamentally beneficial," Kamaleson exhibits a very naive understanding of Liberation Theology that makes his approval of it more comprehensible but no less dangerous in terms of his influence in the evangelical world.

VII. *Critical Analysis of Liberation Theology:*

My article, "Jesus, Habakkuk and Liberation Theology," presents a basic critique of Liberation Theology for laypersons. However there is no doubt that the most devastating criticism of Liberation Theology ever written has come from Rubem Alves, an "insider" who was the father of the movement in many ways. In 1973 Alves wrote "Marxism as the Guarantee of Faith," in which he pulled back the veil on the real story of Marxism's place in Liberation Theology and gave his own reasons for repudiating the movement to which he had helped give birth in the 1960s.

Orlando Costas, the most prominent Protestant historian of the liberationist movement, has offered an insightful critique of Liberation Theology in his book, *The Church and its Mission,* pp. 257ff.

Alfredo Fierro of the University Institute of Theology in Madrid has interspersed criticism of Liberation Theology with that of other political theologies in his excellent work, *The Militant Gospel.*

Samuel Escobar, an important Latin American evangelical leader, has teamed up with other Latin American leaders to produce an in-depth evaluation of Liberation Theology and other theologies in "A Latin American critique of Latin American theology."

Two very helpful Latin American Roman Catholic critiques of Liberation Theology are *Liberation or Revolution?* by Alfonso Lopez Trujillo, the Archbishop of Medellin, Colombia, and head of CELAM, and Bonaventure Kloppenburg's little book, *Temptations for the Theology of Liberation.*

Ronald Nash has compiled a good collection of North American analysis in his edition of *Liberation Theology.*

Perhaps one of the best "critiques" of Liberation Theology written in North America does not even mention it by name. John Yoder's *The Original Revolution* defines Jesus' "revolution" so clearly that it precludes the possibility of a liberationist interpretation of Him. Yoder's discussion of why Jesus rejected the Zealot insurrectionist option of His day is especially appropriate for evaluating Liberation Theology (pp. 21-24).

Finally, German theologian of hope, Jorgen Moltmann, has written "An Open Letter to Jose Miguez Bonino." In it he asks the liberation theologians some very revealing questions, especially about their ties with "the people" of Latin America.

VIII. *Other Branches of Liberation Theology:*

A. Black Liberation Theology:
  The most well-known black liberation theologian is James Cone, whose theology can be studied in his books, *A Black Theology of Liberation, My Soul Looks Back* and *Speaking the Truth.* Another good source is the work of Gayraud Wilmore, which includes *Black Religion and Black Radicalism,* "The Path toward Racial Justice" and *Black Theology* (which he wrote with Cone). One of the most recent additions to this area of study is Josiah Young's book, *Black and African Theologies.*

B. Black African Liberation Theology:
  Louise Kretzchmar's master's thesis for the University of Cambridge, *Black Theology in South Africa,* gives a much-needed overview of this theological movement. In reading the works of black African liberationists, it might be helpful to begin with South African Boesak, who has written *Farewell to Innocence, The Finger of God* and *Walking on Thorns.* Also, John Mbiti's *The Concept of God in Africa* and Desmond Tutu's *Crying in the Wilderness, Hope and Suffering* and "The Theology of Liberation in Africa," as well as Chukwudum Okolo's "Liberation Theology and the African Church" will prove useful for understanding this theology.

C. Feminist Liberation Theology:
  The primary feminist liberation theologian is Rosemary Ruether whose books, *Liberation Theology, The Radical Kingdom* and *Womanguides,* give a very adequate introduction to the use of liberationist thought from a feminist perspective. Letty Russel, a lesser-known but very strong feminist liberation theologian, explains her own approach to theology in *Human Liberation in a Feminist Perspective.*

D. Minjung Liberation Theology:

Korea has spawned its own brand of Liberation Theology called "Minjung Theology" (or Theology of the People). Younghak Hyun's article, "Minjung theology and the religion of Han" offers a profitable introduction to this uniquely Korean variety of Liberation Theology.

IX. *Related Subjects:*
The study of Liberation Theology opens the door to the study of many related themes that are linked with liberationist thinking:

A. Base Community Churches:
Among Roman Catholics in Latin America an innovative approach to church life is the "comunidades de base" (for which "base communities" is a very inadequate translation). These new, small-group, grassroots churches are springing up all over Latin America, especially in Brazil. In general they meet to pray for one another, read the Scriptures with a liberationist interpretation and plan community projects of solidarity with the poor and opposition to oppressors. Leonardo Boff's controversial work, *Ecclesiogenesis,* is probably the best defense of these groups, along with Sergio Torres' *The Challenge of Basic Christian Communities.* Those looking for a scholarly, comprehensive study of this phenomenon should read the book based on William Cook's doctoral dissertation for Fuller Theological Seminary, *The Expectation of the Poor.* Cook grew up as the son of missionaries to Latin America and has worked for many years in Central and South America as a missionary. For a brief discussion of base community churches, see Joao Batista Libanio's "BECs in Sociocultural Perspective."

B. Christians for Socialism:
This ecumenical movement, which brought together more than 400 Latin American liberationists, produced the clearest, most radical expression of Liberation Theology ever published. John Eagleson describes the

Encounter of 1972 and translates the entire text of conclusions in his work, *Christians and Socialism.*

C. Violence:

Central to the study of Liberation Theology is the question of whether a Christian can be involved in acts of violence, even for a good purpose. Liberationists Rubem Alves ("Violence and Counterviolence") and Jose Miguez Bonino ("Violence, a theological reflection") present the traditional liberationist argument in favor of Christians using violence for humanizing revolution. A fascinating response to many of their arguments is found in Jacques Ellul's *Violence,* which is extremely thought-provoking. Os Guinness outlines modern views of violence in his book, *Violence.*

D. Secularization:

One evaluation of Liberation Theology sees it as another in a series of attempts to "secularize Christianity," to remove the supernatural and religious elements from Christianity and reduce it to just another ideological or political view. British theologian E. L. Mascall has written the classic work on this subject, *The Secularisation of Christianity.*

A more popular (and not quite so cautious) expression of this idea is presented in the controversial book based on Edward Norman's B. B. C. Reith Lectures of 1978, *Christianity and the World Order.* In it Norman decries the politicization of Christianity in Liberation Theology, the World Council of Churches and other Christian forums. For a strident criticism of Norman's views, see *Christian Faith and Political Hopes,* edited by Hadden Willmer of Leeds University, and Andrew Kirk's "Edward Norman and political involvement."

E. Marxism:

Several works listed in the bibliography will aid those interested in studying more about Marxism. Klaus Bockmuehl's book, *The Challenge of Marxism,* gives an evangelical Christian response to the main tenets of

Marxist theory.

Edgar Bundy's *The Marxist-Revolutionary Invasion of the Latin American Churches* comes across a bit too "hot-headed" but has excellent documentation.

Andrew Kirk's article, "The Meaning of Man in the Debate between Christianity and Marxism," highlights the contradictory worldviews involved in the two systems. His "Marxism and the Church in Latin America" shows Marxist influence in Latin American life.

Rubem Alves expresses his belief that the Marxist/Christian synthesis can only damage both systems in his article, "Marxism as the Guarantee of Faith."

Brian Griffith's *Is Revolution Change?* challenges the whole logic of Marxist revolution.

Jose Miguez Bonino's book, *Christians and Marxists,* contains one of the most extensive discussions of the relationship between Christians and Marxists of any liberationist writings.

Jose Porfirio Miranda devotes *Marx and the Bible* to the exposition of 12 proofs of the oneness of Christianity and Marxism. In *Marx against the Marxists* he attempts to prove that Marx was actually a Christian who believed in God when he elaborated his theories.

Michael Novak's *The Spirit of Democratic Capitalism* argues quite convincingly for the superiority of capitalism over socialism.

In John Hutchinson's *Christian Faith and Social Action* Reinhold Niebuhr contributes a very revealing essay explaining why he changed from a pro-Marxist to an adamantly anti-Marxist position.

Finally, Chris Wigglesworth, who came to evangelical faith out of Marxism, gives some well-informed analysis of Marxism in his article, "Which Way to Utopia: with Marx or Jesus?"

X. *Alternatives to Liberation Theology:*

No study of Liberation Theology would be complete without a careful consideration of the alternatives to this theology's formula for social change if violent revolution is to be rejected. It is unfair to take away a possible solution to the misery and suffering of Latin America (and of all the Third World) without offering a viable alternative. Here my own preferences will be quite evident as I describe some of the most laudable presentations of workable alternatives for solving these problems from an evangelical perspective.

The evangelical revivals in mid-19th century America are seen to have produced peaceful social change on a grand scale according to Timothy Smith's scholarly work, *Revivalism and Social Reform*. This proves that strong, evangelistic, evangelical faith can be united with effective social action in a successful campaign for social change. The reality of this union of evangelism and social ministry has been brought out as one of the hallmarks of the Wesleyan revival in Bernard Semmel's *The Methodist Revolution* and Howard Snyder's *The Radical Wesley*. The similarity of the social situation in Wesley's day and the threat of imminent revolution to redress the abuses of 18th century capitalism make the Wesleyan model of evangelism and social ministry of crucial interest in the contemporary Latin American situation.

The last 10 years have seen a dramatic increase in evangelical thinking, writing and action regarding bringing evangelism and social responsibility together. John Stott's edition of *The Lausanne Covenant* evidences a new evangelical awareness of past deficiencies in social ministry and a genuine commitment to correct that imbalance. The pamphlet, *Evangelism and Social Responsibility,* indicates the unanimity of the delegates to the combined Lausanne Committee on World Evangelization/World Evangelical Fellowship consultation of 1982 in asserting the need for an integral, holistic evangelical ministry. It also demonstrates their differing opinions regarding Christian participation in efforts to radically change the structure of society (referred to as the difference between "social service" and "social action" in the document).

Bruce Nicholls, who until 1986 was the executive secretary of the Theological Commission of the World

Evangelical Fellowship, has edited two significant works dealing with these concerns from evangelical perspectives, *The Church: God's Agent for Change* and *In Word and Deed: Evangelism and Social Responsibility,* which contain articles by well-known evangelical leaders such as: Peter Kuzmic of Yugoslavia, Theodore Williams of India, Tokunbok Adeyemo of Kenya, Jonathan Chao of Hong Kong, Joseph Ton of Romania, Bong Rin Ro of Tawian, David Bosch of South Africa, Ron Sider of the United States and Peter Beyerhaus of West Germany.

This increased literary activity among evangelicals runs parallel to increasing evangelical social service and action, although the literary "smoke" may be more voluminous than the actual social ministry "fire." Ron Sider's books, *Evangelicals and Development* (ed.), *Rich Christians in an Age of Hunger* and *Evangelism, Salvation and Social Justice* (ed.), have the goal of mobilizing Christians for more effective social action.

One evangelical who has been writing for some time on the issue of evangelical social action is Mennonite John Yoder. Reading four of his books in chronological order will give a good view of how his concepts have developed. They are: *The Original Revolution* (1971), *The Politics of Jesus* (1972), *Christian Witness to the State* (1977) and *The Priestly Kingdom* (1986). His views on how Christians can best affect their societies have been very influential in many evangelical circles.

Finally we must return to Emilio Nunez, who ends his excellent book, *Liberation Theology,* by describing a holistic approach to "evangelical praxis" for Latin America (pp. 177-190), which is very similar to the last chapter of this book. Nunez' call for a *biblical* base for Christian social action in Latin America is indicative of the way Latin American evangelicals, responding to the excesses of the liberationists, have "rediscovered" the dual biblical mandate to preach the gospel and serve those who are in need. I pray that the entire Church will make this discovery as we confront the challenge of Liberation Theology around the world.